Usborne

MY FIRST ENCYCLOPEDIA

Usborne

MY FIRST ENCYCLOPEDIA

Written by Matthew Oldham, Emily Bone, Alex Frith,
Alice James, Minna Lacey & Abigail Wheatley

Illustrated by Lee Cosgrove, Tony Neal & Jane Newland

Designed by Alice Reese

Contents

Our world

pages 6-37

From steamy jungles to scorching deserts and deep blue oceans, our world is full of wonderful places, plants and animals to discover...

Space

pages 38-71

Explore beyond our planet, among speeding spacecraft, hurtling space rocks, vast planets and sparkling stars.

Science

pages 72-97

What makes things move? How do ears hear? Which things sink or float? Discover the answers, and lots more fascinating questions...

My body

pages 98-129

Your body is amazing. Find out about your brilliant brain, stretchy muscles, super senses and other parts that work together to keep you going.

Animals

pages 130-161

Enter the astonishing world of animals, from big, furry, fierce ones to tiny, shy, smooth ones, and absolutely everything in between.

Dinosaurs

pages 162-183

Long, long ago, mighty dinosaurs roamed the land. Discover how big they were, what they ate, and why they aren't here any more.

Long ago

pages 184-215

Voyage with Viking raiders, explore a bustling market in Timbuktu and meet the people who first invented toilet paper...

Index

pages 216-224

Here you'll find a list of all the important words in this book, and where to find them.

Usborne Quicklinks

For links to websites where you can discover more about the topics in this book with videos, online activities and fun things to try at home, go to **usborne.com/Quicklinks** and type in the title of this book. Children should be supervised online. Turn to page 224 to find out more.

Our world

Our world, our home

From the bluest oceans to the tallest mountains, our world is full of spectacular sights. Wherever you live, it's outside your door, waiting to be explored...

As it spins, some parts of the Earth catch the Sun's light, but others are in shadow.

Maria lives in Brazil.

Fergus lives in Australia.

When it's day for Maria, it's night for Fergus.

When it's night for Maria, it's day for Fergus.

Changing seasons

Seasons are changes in the weather that take place at different times of the year. Some parts of the world have four seasons, others only have two.

In spring, flowers come out and lots of animals have babies.

Summer is the warmest season. Fruits and crops start to ripen.

In autumn, many leaves turn crimson and golden as the weather cools.

Winter is the coldest season. Some animals spend it asleep.

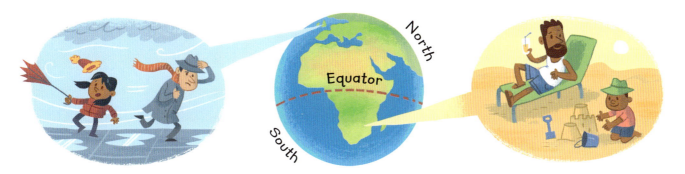

Earth is divided into North and South by an imaginary line around the middle called the Equator. When it's winter in the North, it's summer in the South.

Seasons change less near the Equator, where the weather is warm all year round. There's often a dry season...

...followed by a wet season, when it rains nearly every day.

Dusty deserts

Deserts are among the driest places on Earth and some can also be the hottest. Living things here have found clever ways to live in the heat, without much water.

Dried up soil turns into dust and sand that blows into big hills called sand dunes.

Falcon for hunting

Sand cat

Fennec foxes

This is an oasis, a small area of the desert where water is found.

Tents which pack up easily

Long robes to cover up from the Sun

Camels for carrying water and possessions

These people live in the Arabian Desert.
They travel around in groups called caravans to find food and water.

These creatures all live in the Mojave Desert in America.
They come out at night, to avoid the heat of the day.

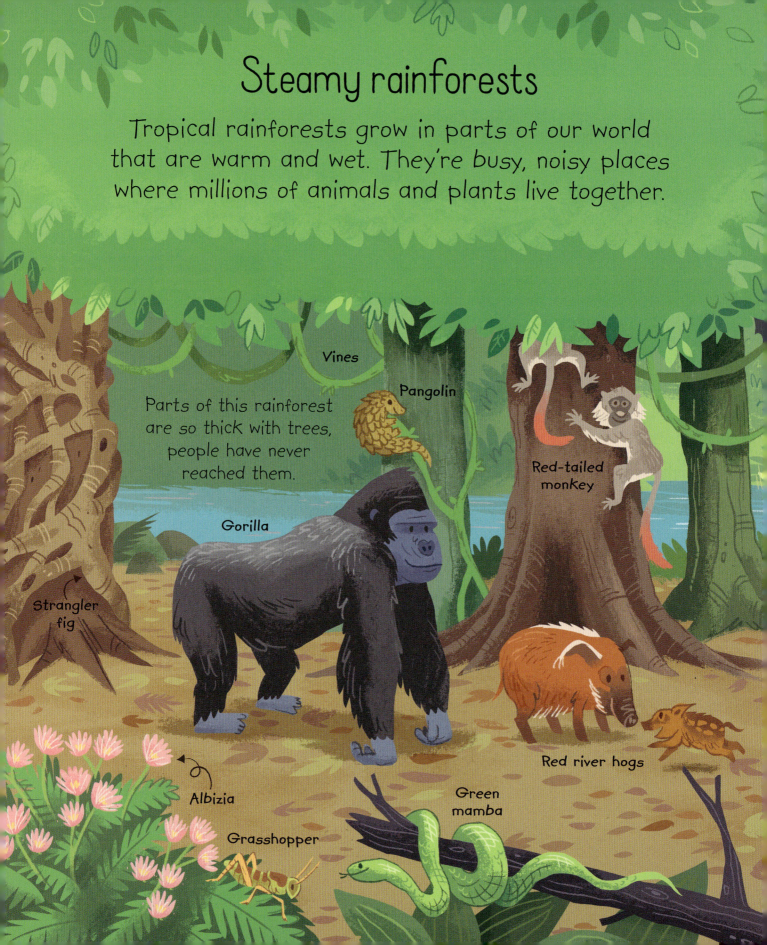

Frozen poles

The North and South Poles are the coldest parts of the planet. The land and sea close to the poles are covered in snow and ice all year.

The area around the South Pole is covered by a vast stretch of land called Antarctica. Most living things are found on the edge of this land, in or near the sea.

The area around the North Pole is called the Arctic. It's mostly covered by a frozen ocean. Many creatures that live here have a lot of body fat and thick fur to keep warm.

The Inuit people live in the Arctic parts of Canada, Alaska and Greenland.

Some Inuit people build temporary shelters called igloos out of snow.

Mountain high

Mountains are the highest places on Earth. They're so high, the weather at the bottom, or base, can be very different from the weather at the top, or peak.

The coldest part of a mountain is the peak. Not many things live here.

Mountain peak

Some mountain peaks stay cold enough for snow all year round.

Ski lift

Snow line

The higher slopes are too cold for trees to grow.

Over time, pieces of rock fall down to form a scree slope.

Scree slope

Pine trees

Lake

When the snow and ice at the top melt, they trickle down to form lakes at the base.

In winter, lots of mountains are entirely covered in snow.

In summer, most of the snow melts. Lots of plants and animals come out.

Valley

Near its start, a river is narrow and flows fast.

Rain and melted snow trickle down from steep slopes.

Often two rivers join together.

When a river flows over a steep step, it makes a waterfall.

Wetland

Kayaks

Paddle steamer

As a river widens, it starts to flow more slowly, making giant bends.

Here are some of the creatures that live in rivers.

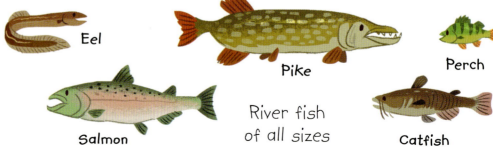

Eel

Pike

Perch

Salmon

River fish of all sizes

Catfish

Running rivers

Even the widest river begins as a narrow stream on a hill. A river always flows downhill, collecting more water along its way. It ends when it meets another river, a lake or the sea.

The coast

The place where land meets the sea is called the coast. Here you might find cliffs, beaches and all sorts of sealife.

The seashells that wash up onto the coast are the remains of different sea creatures.

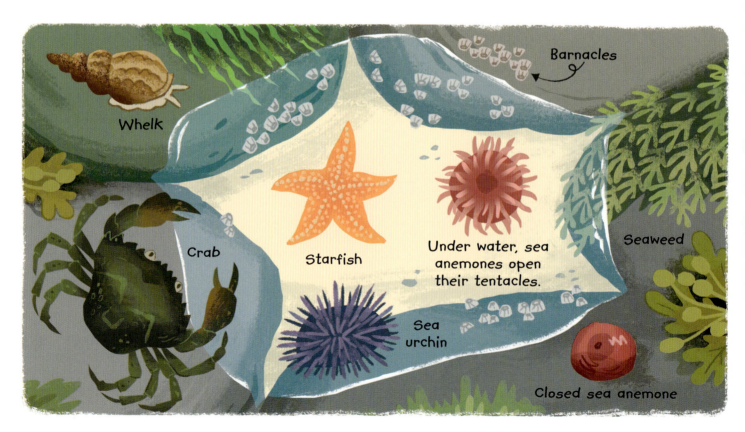

Pools are left behind when waves wash over the rocks.

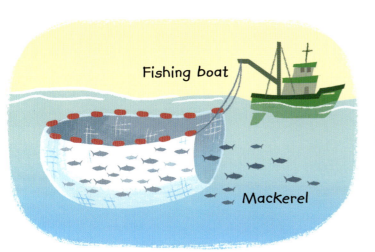

The oceans provide food for people all over our world.

Some sea creatures need to come to the surface to breathe.

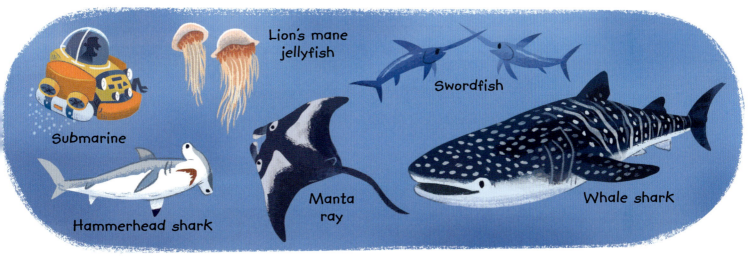

Scientists travel in underwater ships called submarines to study sea creatures.

Parts of the ocean are so deep that sunlight can't reach the bottom.

Under the ground

The world beneath our feet is full of life and buzzing with activity, just as it is on the surface.

Volcanoes

Volcanoes are openings in the Earth's surface. Sometimes the hot sticky rock that's buried deep underneath bursts through, causing a big explosion known as an eruption.

This volcano is erupting.

Hot gases

Clouds of ash

The red-hot rock that's forced out is called lava.

Blocks of solid rock

When lava cools, it becomes solid rock.

Lava

Some lava is runny and flows quickly. Other lava is lumpy and flows slowly.

Earthquakes

The ground beneath our feet is usually firm and solid, but during an earthquake it can tremble and shake.

Most earthquakes...

...only happen in certain parts of the world.

...only last for a few seconds.

...aren't dangerous or even noticeable.

But some earthquakes are more powerful.

They can shake whole buildings...

...or even make them fall down.

In places where earthquakes happen often, people know how to prepare for the bigger ones...

Indoors, it's safest to shelter under a table while you hold on to it.

Outdoors, it's safest to stay in the open, away from buildings and trees.

Earthquakes at sea can cause giant waves called tsunamis. They can flow for long distances inland, flooding towns and ruining crops.

Wild weather

Storms look different all over the world. The most powerful storms don't happen often, but when they strike, they show the weather at its wildest.

In dry places, dust storms can blow sand for thousands of miles.

In cold parts of the world, blizzards can cover huge areas in thick layers of snow.

Tornadoes are winds that spin around very fast to make funnel-shaped clouds.

Some storms are so big you can even see them from space. They look like huge swirls

Living in our world

The Earth provides for us in lots of ways. It has everything we need to survive, but we must look after what we have so it doesn't run out.

We eat fish from the sea.

Most of our food comes from farms.

Drinking water comes from springs, rivers and lakes.

Metals and stones are used to make things.

Paper and wood come from trees.

Glass is made from baked sand.

Bricks are made from baked clay.

The Earth gives us food to eat and water to drink. It also gives us materials we can use to make things and build houses.

Burning fuel gives us energy and creates electricity, but it can make the air dirty. We also use some cleaner energy sources to make electricity.

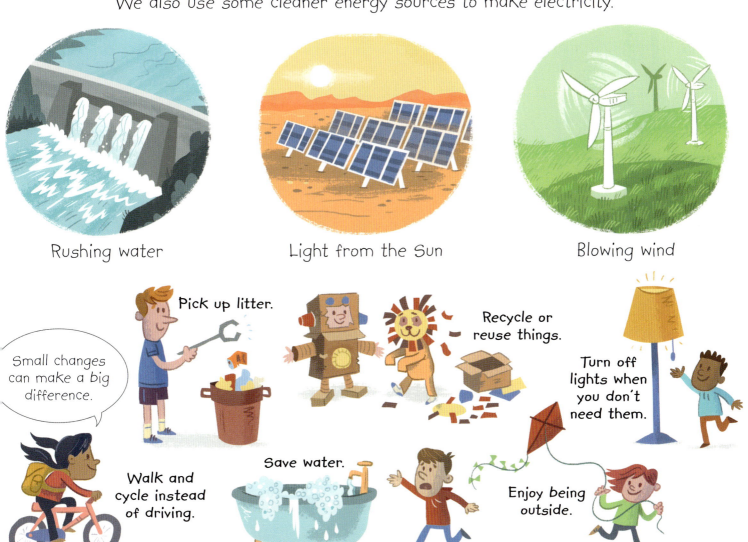

There's a lot you can do to look after our world.

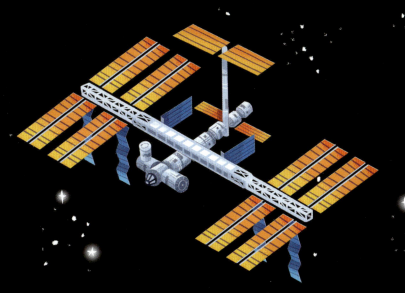

Space

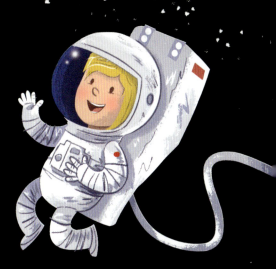

The night sky

When the Sun sets, the sky grows dark. You'll start to see twinkling stars. What you're looking at is just a tiny part of SPACE.

Space is so enormous, no one knows how big it really is.

Someone who studies space is called an astronomer.

What is space?

We live on planet Earth. Space is everything around our planet. There are lots of incredible things out there.

Moons

Planets

Stars

Galaxies

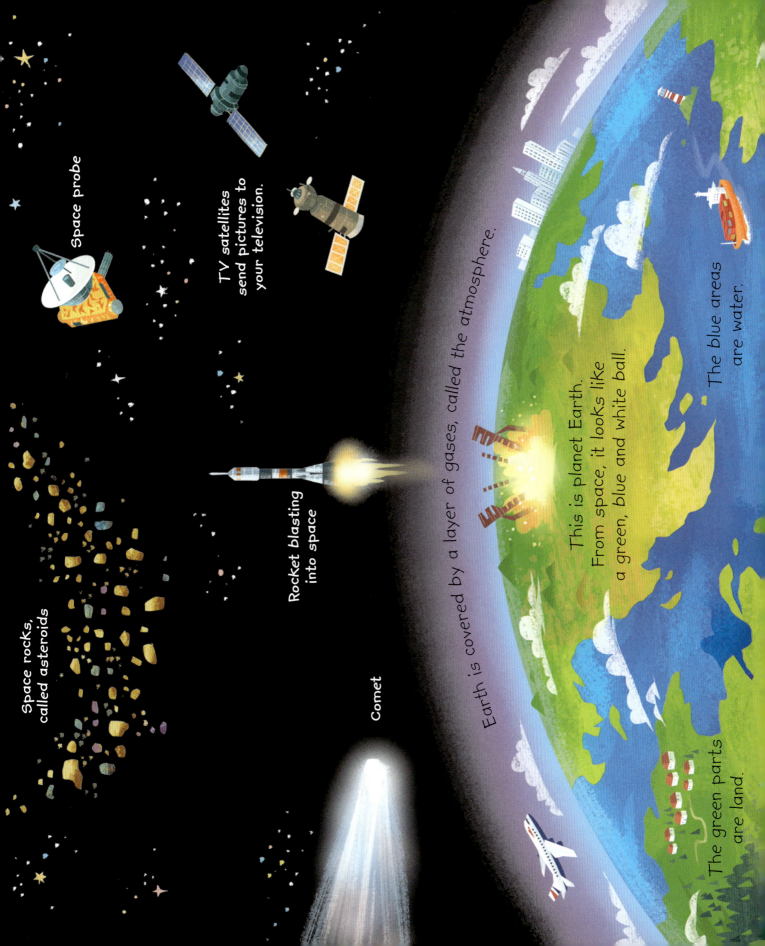

The Moon

The Moon is a big ball of rock that travels around the Earth.

The lighter areas are the tops of high mountains.

There's no air or water, and nothing lives on the Moon.

The dark patches are huge holes, called craters.

Space school

Before astronauts go into space, they have to do a lot of training.

Learning everything about space and space travel

Getting very fit and being tested on it

Finding out how to work spacecraft controls

Emergency escape drills

Learning what to do if they crash into the sea

Using tools

Learning the languages of astronauts from different countries

Talking to experienced astronauts

Repairing a pretend spacecraft while floating in a huge water tank

Being given a mission and meeting the rest of the crew

Lift-off!

A rocket, called a launch vehicle, flies a team of three astronauts into space.

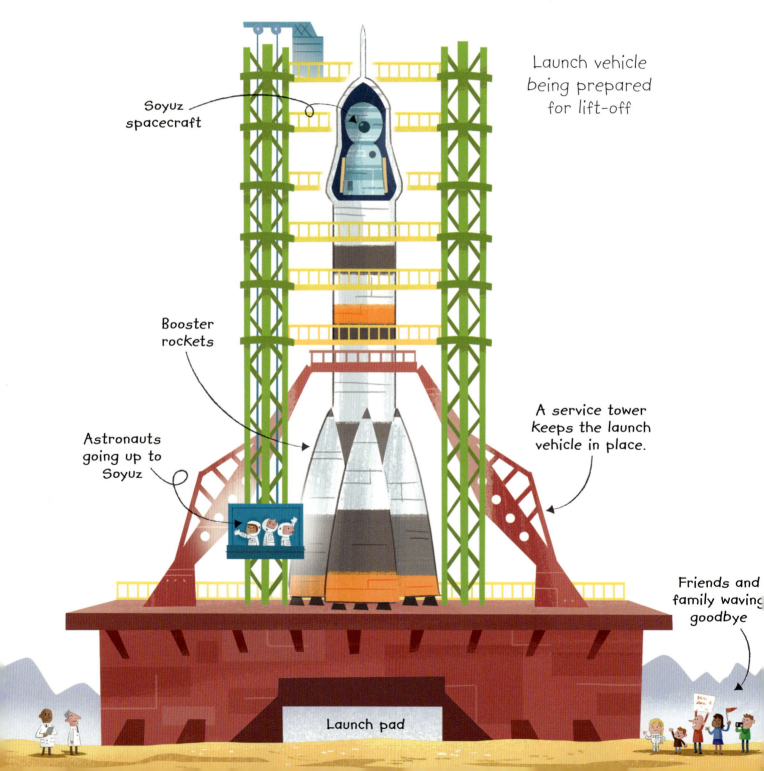

Astronauts inside Soyuz getting ready for lift-off

Booster rockets firing

LIFT-OFF!

Booster rockets falling back to Earth

Launch vehicle falling back and Soyuz flying away

Space station

In space, astronauts live and work in a spacecraft called the International Space Station. It flies high above the Earth.

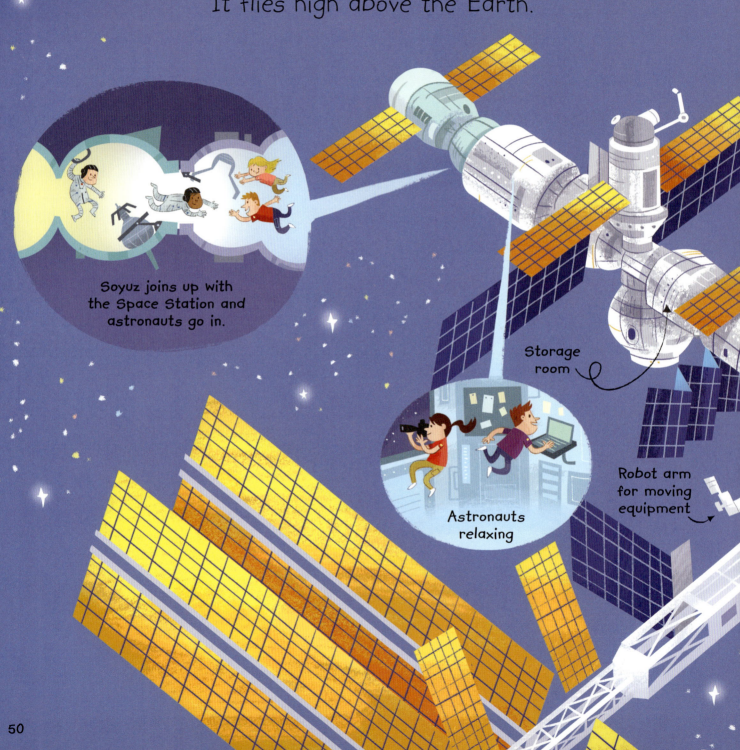

Soyuz joins up with the Space Station and astronauts go in.

Storage room

Astronauts relaxing

Robot arm for moving equipment

Living in space

On the Space Station, everything floats.
This is what happens during a day:

Washing using dry shampoo

Using the toilet

Exercising for two hours

Most food comes in packets.

Eating

Repairing the outside of the Space Station

Doing experiments

Relaxing

Cleaning

Receiving deliveries from supply spacecraft

Unpacking supplies

Talking to family back home

Taking photos of Earth

Going to sleep

Spacewalk

There's no air in space. When astronauts go on a spacewalk outside the Space Station, they have to wear a space suit that gives them air and keeps them safe.

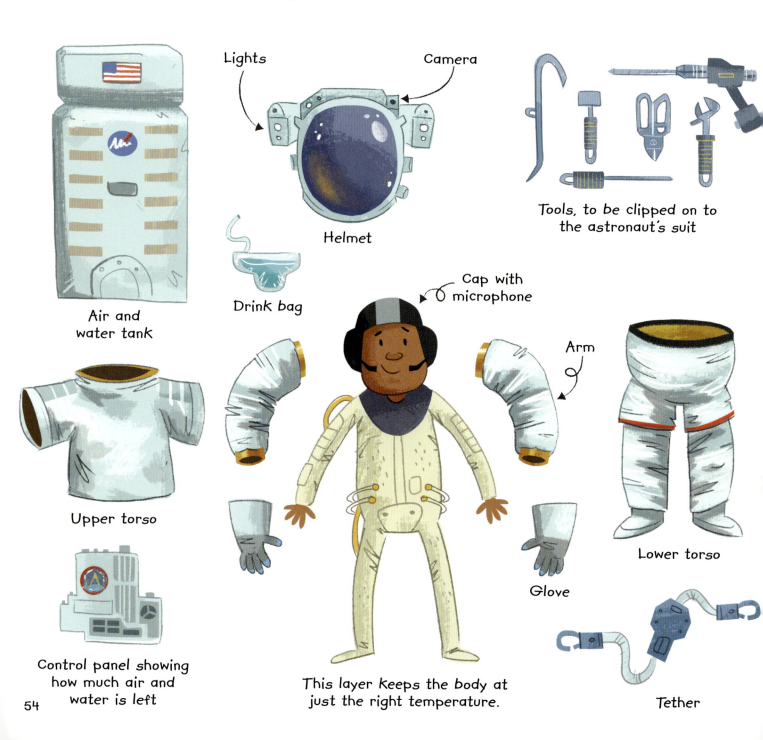

Astronauts go on spacewalks in pairs.

Checking spacesuits and putting them on

Going into an airlock for 24 hours

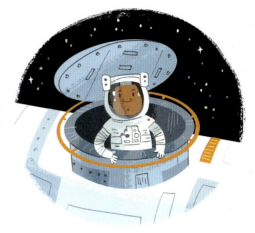
Opening the exit hatch

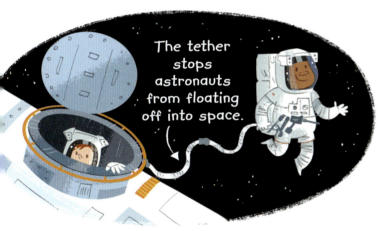
Attaching the tether and going outside

Receiving instructions from Earth

Fitting new equipment to the Space Station

Drinking from the drink bag

Returning to the Space Station

The Solar System

The Earth is one of eight planets that travel around the Sun. The Sun and the planets are known as the Solar System.

Mercury

Earth

This is the Moon. Other planets have moons, too.

The Sun

Sometimes, space rocks crash into planets.

Venus

Venus is covered in thick, poisonous clouds.

Mars

Jupiter

Jupiter is the biggest planet. It has more than 60 moons.

The Great Red Spot is a huge storm.

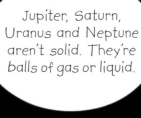

Jupiter, Saturn, Uranus and Neptune aren't solid. They're balls of gas or liquid.

Neptune

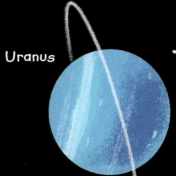

Uranus

Uranus has rings made from ice and dust.

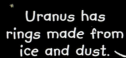

The Asteroid Belt is a big group of space rocks.

A comet is a ball of gas, ice and dust.

It leaves a bright tail behind it.

This is Pluto. It's a dwarf planet.

Saturn

Saturn's rings are made from chunks of rock and ice.

Exploring Mars

Small spacecraft have flown vehicles, called rovers, to Mars. Rovers find out more about the rocks and air on Mars.

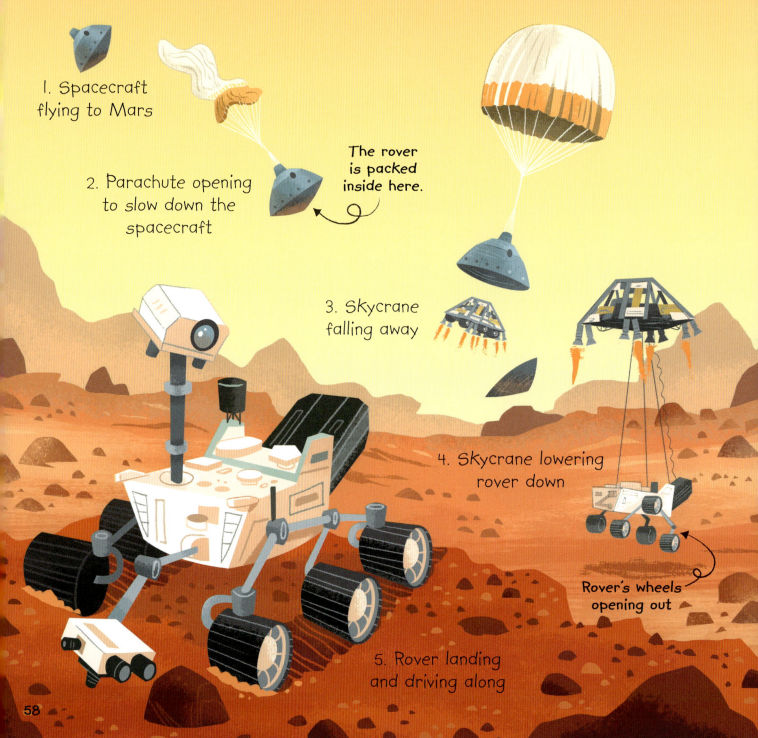

1. Spacecraft flying to Mars
2. Parachute opening to slow down the spacecraft

The rover is packed inside here.

3. Skycrane falling away
4. Skycrane lowering rover down

Rover's wheels opening out

5. Rover landing and driving along

Receiving instructions from Earth

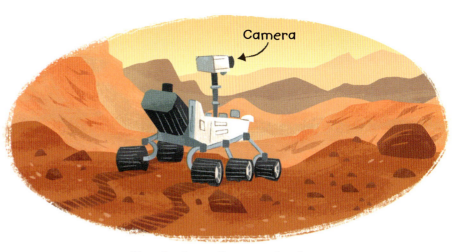

Exploring different places and taking pictures

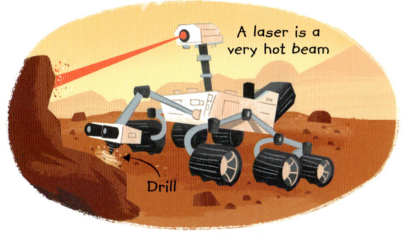

Firing a laser and drilling into rocks to find out what's inside them

Scooping up dust and testing it

Finding out about the weather on Mars

Sending pictures back to Earth

Stars

Stars are massive balls of very, very hot gases. The Sun is a star. This is what it looks like close up.

Gases bubbling on the Sun's surface

This is a solar flare, a big explosion.

From Earth, the Sun looks bigger than other stars because it's our closest star.

There are different types of stars.

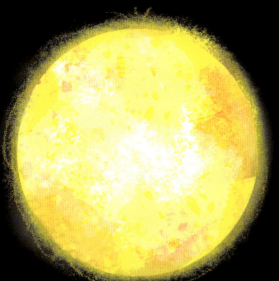

Our Sun is a type of star called a yellow dwarf.

The biggest and most powerful stars are called supergiants.

The least powerful stars are called red dwarfs.

Life of a star

A new star is formed out of a huge, swirling cloud of gas and dust called a nebula.

This is the Tarantula Nebula.

1. Part of the nebula gets thicker and hotter.

2. Slowly, it turns into a hot ball.

3. This becomes a new star.

Stars glow and burn for millions and millions of years. Then, they start to change.

"Different stars change in different ways."

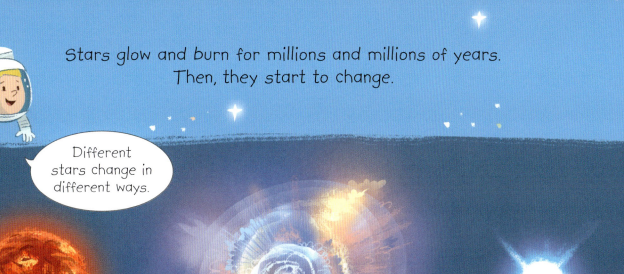

1. A yellow dwarf star gets cooler, bigger and duller.

2. Its outer layers puff away.

3. Eventually, a white dwarf star is left behind.

1. A supergiant star gets bigger and brighter.

2. It explodes. This is called a supernova.

3. A big cloud of gas is left behind.

Great galaxies

Millions and millions of stars form massive groups, called galaxies. Galaxies come in different shapes and sizes.

This is a spiral galaxy.

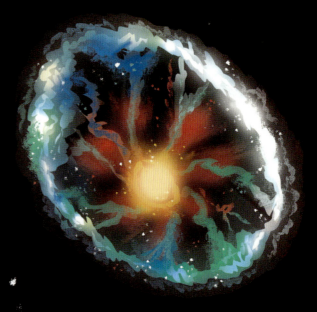

This is called the Cartwheel Galaxy, because it looks like a wheel.

Some galaxies look like bright balls.

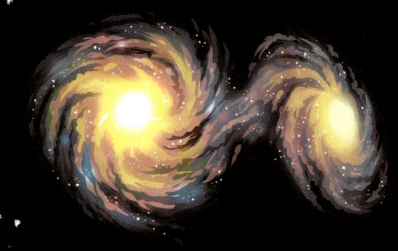

Other galaxies are slowly joining together.

Hubble is a famous space telescope.

A spacecraft taking Hubble into space

Hubble flying around the Earth

Astronauts have been sent to make repairs.

Astronauts fitting new cameras onto Hubble

Radio dishes on Earth collect the pictures, then send them to computers.

Hubble taking lots of pictures and sending them back to Earth

Each swirl and dot in this picture is a faraway galaxy.

Scientists studying the pictures

Stargazing

The best time to see stars is on a cloudless night when the moon isn't too bright.

It can be cold at night, so wrap up warm. It's more comfortable if you lie or sit on a blanket. Bring snacks and hot drinks.

Stars look like tiny points of light in the sky.

But really they're huge balls of fire, like the Sun.

The Sun is the closest star. Other stars are very far away.

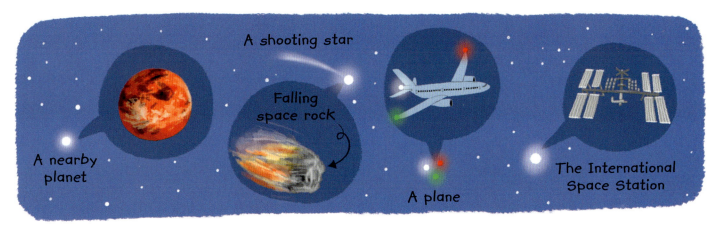

Some of the things shining in the night sky aren't stars at all.

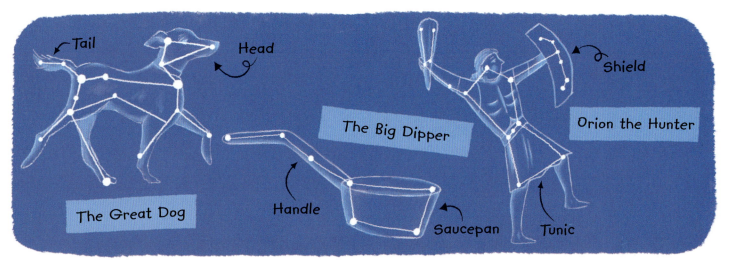

Ancient stargazers joined up some stars with imaginary lines to make pictures called constellations. These are just a few of them.

What you can see in the sky depends on where you are and what time of year it is.

Moon watching

The Moon is usually easy to spot in the night sky, but it looks different at different times. If you look carefully, you can see pale and dark patches on its surface.

When the Moon looks like this, it's called a Full Moon.

These pale spots are holes known as craters.

These dark patches are called seas, but really they're smooth rock.

You can get a good view of the Moon through binoculars or a telescope.

The Moon looks different at different times. Over a month, it goes from a New Moon to a Full Moon, and back again.

When the Moon is close to the horizon, it sometimes looks yellow.

On cold nights you can sometimes see a pale ring around the Moon.

When the Moon shines brightly, it makes shadows on the ground.

Science

What is science?

Science is about the world around us. It teaches us about nearly everything – from what goes on inside our bodies, to the air we breathe, to faraway planets.

People who study science are called scientists.

"What do magnets do?"

"How do they work?"

Their work often starts with lots of questions.

Next they think of ideas about how to answer these questions.

"The magnet only picks up the fork."

Then they try out the ideas by doing tests called experiments.

This is a laboratory, a room where scientists carry out experiments.

Light and dark

Different things make light.
Without it, people wouldn't be able to
see and everything would be DARK.

During the day the Sun
lights up the world.

At night, twinkling stars
shine in the sky.

When things burn,
they give us light.

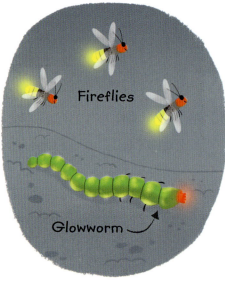

Some living things can
make their own light.

People can use electricity
to make light, too.

When an object blocks out light, it makes a shadow.

If the object moves closer to the light, the shadow becomes bigger and fuzzier.

The Sun makes a rainbow when it shines through drops of water.

When the Sun shines through rain, a big rainbow can appear in the sky.

Reflections happen when light hits something shiny and bounces off it again.

Sounds all around

There are many different sounds in the world around you. You hear sounds when they reach your ears.

There are quiet sounds...

and there are loud sounds.

If a sound is very loud, you might feel it buzzing.

Sounds grow louder and louder as you get closer to them.

Sometimes you can hear a sound before you see what's made it.

Sounds happen when something makes the air wobble.

The air wobbles a tiny bone inside your ear.

Your brain recognizes the wobbling as a sound.

Air everywhere

Air is all around us. You can't see it,
but sometimes you can feel it.

You can feel air when
you breathe out.

When the wind blows,
you can feel rushing air.

You can also feel rushing air
if you move quickly.

Some things can float in air. These balloons are filled with something called helium.
Helium is lighter than air. That makes the balloons float.

When things fall to the ground, the air rushes past them.

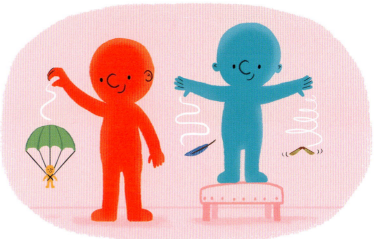

Some things catch the air as they fall. This makes them fall more slowly.

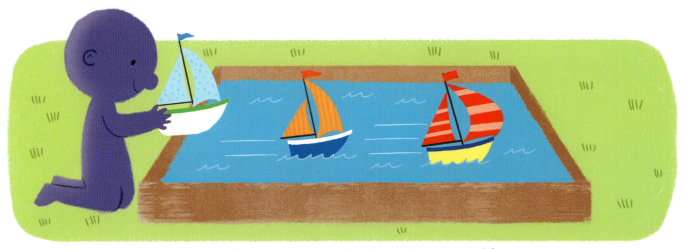

These sails catch the air when the wind blows. This pushes the boats along.

"Paper planes can glide through the air."

"Mine has big, wide wings so it stays in the air for longer."

The bigger and flatter something is, the more air it can catch.

What are things made of?

Everything in the world is made from different types of stuff called materials. Different materials can do different things.

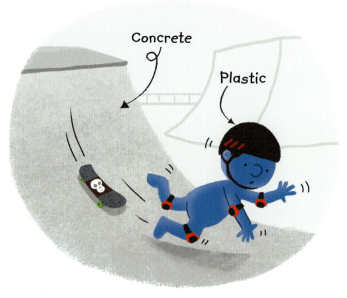

Some types of materials are hard.

Some types of materials are soft.

Some types of materials are light.

Some types of materials are heavy.

Some types of materials can stretch or bend, but others are stiff.

Some types of materials soak up water.

Some types of materials keep water out.

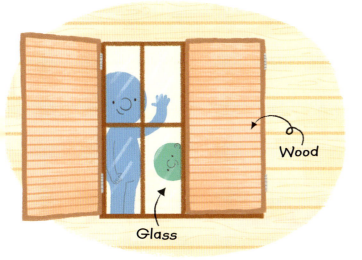

Some types of materials are see-through, and some aren't.

Many materials we use come from the natural world, but some, such as plastic, are made by people.

Floating and sinking

When you put different materials in water, some of them float near the top, and some of them sink to the bottom.

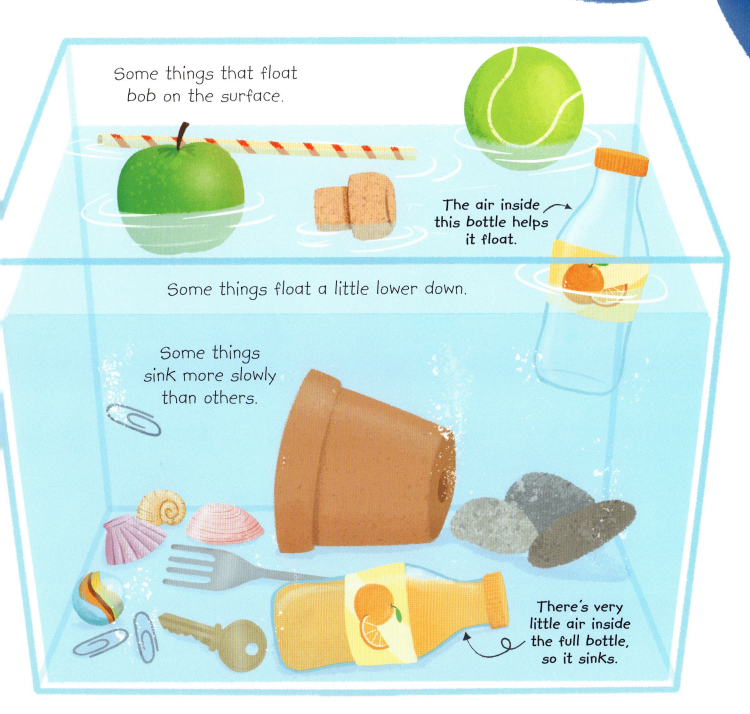

How things change

Materials can change. Sometimes they can change when they're mixed with other materials. Sometimes they can change if they get hot or cold.

Mixing two different materials can make them change.

Soap mixes with water to make a bubbly foam.

Sugar disappears when it mixes with water.

You can make cream fluffy by mixing air into it with a whisk.

Powdery flour mixes with water and other ingredients to make dough.

Some things don't mix together easily. The oil in salad dressing floats on top of the vinegar.

Some materials change if you heat them up but change back again when they cool down.

Some materials change if you cool them down but change back again when they warm up.

Some materials change if you heat them up, and they don't change back – even when they cool down.

The world of plants

Plants are living things that come in many shapes and sizes – from swishing grasses and tangled bushes to enormous, towering trees.

Plants need air, water and sunlight to grow.

Leaves soak up sunlight. They use energy from the Sun to make food.

Some leaves are wide and flat.

Some leaves look like spiky needles or sharp scales.

Nearly all plants have roots that grow down into the ground.

How a seed grows

Many plants grow from tiny seeds. This is a sunflower seed.

The seed cracks. A tiny root appears.

A shoot pushes above the soil and leaves sprout.

Branches

Most plants grow flowers.

Nuts

Flowers make fruits.

Fruits contain seeds.

Tree trunk

Flowers

Some fruits are soft and juicy.

Berries

Some fruits are dry and hard, such as nuts.

Roots

Roots keep plants firmly in the ground.

Roots also suck up water from the soil.

The plant grows bigger. More leaves and a flower bud appear.

The flower opens and seeds form in the middle.

The flower fades. Seeds fall to the ground, ready to grow again.

Trees and leaves

Trees and their leaves grow in many shapes and sizes.

Some trees are tall and thin...

some have wide spreading branches...

and some have a pointed shape.

Trees that lose all their leaves in winter are called deciduous.

Trees that keep their leaves all year are called evergreen.

Apple trees are deciduous. This is how they change through the year.

Different trees have different types of leaves, fruits and seeds.

All about flowers

Flowers come in many shapes and sizes.
They help plants to make seeds, so new plants can grow.

Some flowers grow on stalks... some on bushy plants... and some on trees.

Different flowers come out at different times of the year.

Some flowers, such as California poppies, turn to face the Sun as it moves across the sky.

Making things move

There are many different ways to make things move, but they all use something called FORCE.

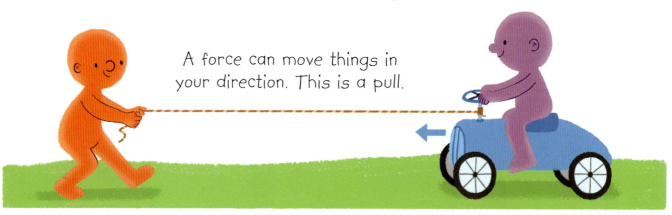

A force can move things in your direction. This is a pull.

A force can also move things away from you. This is a push.

The less force you use to move something, the slower it goes.

If you use MORE force, it will go more quickly.

Some forces work by touching the thing they're moving...

even if you can't see this happening.

Some forces work without touching anything. Magnets push and pull on some things, even if they're not touching them.

An invisible force called gravity pulls things down to the ground without touching them.

It's gravity that pulls this toy car down the slope, too.

Experiments to try

A great way to learn more about science is to do some experiments yourself. Ask a grown-up for help before you start.

Beating heart

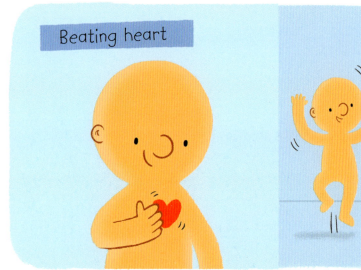

1. You can feel your heart beat by touching your chest.

2. Jump up and down for a minute.

3. Feel your heart beat again. Is it faster or slower?

Mixing together

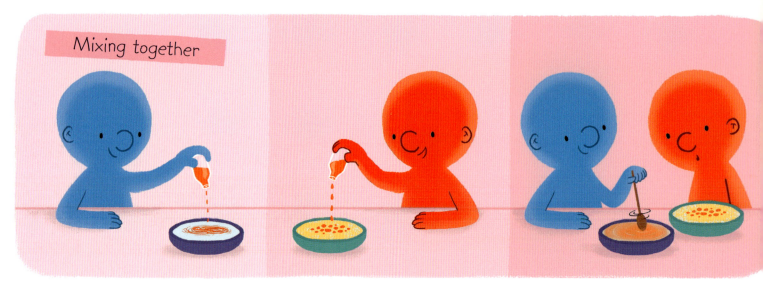

1. Drop some liquid food dye into some water.

2. Drop some of the food dye into some oil.

3. Stir each mixture. Can you see a difference?

Sprouting carrot

1. Ask a grown-up to cut the top off a carrot.
2. Put the carrot top on a saucer with some water.
3. Leave in a sunny place and check every day.

Musical bottles

1. Take two empty bottles of the same shape and size.
2. Fill one of the bottles with water.
3. Blow over each bottle. Can you hear a difference?

> Science experiments don't always go the way you expect. If something surprises you, do the experiment again. If you're still surprised, try to explain what you see.

My body

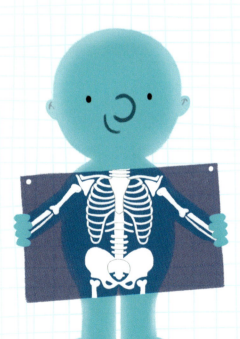

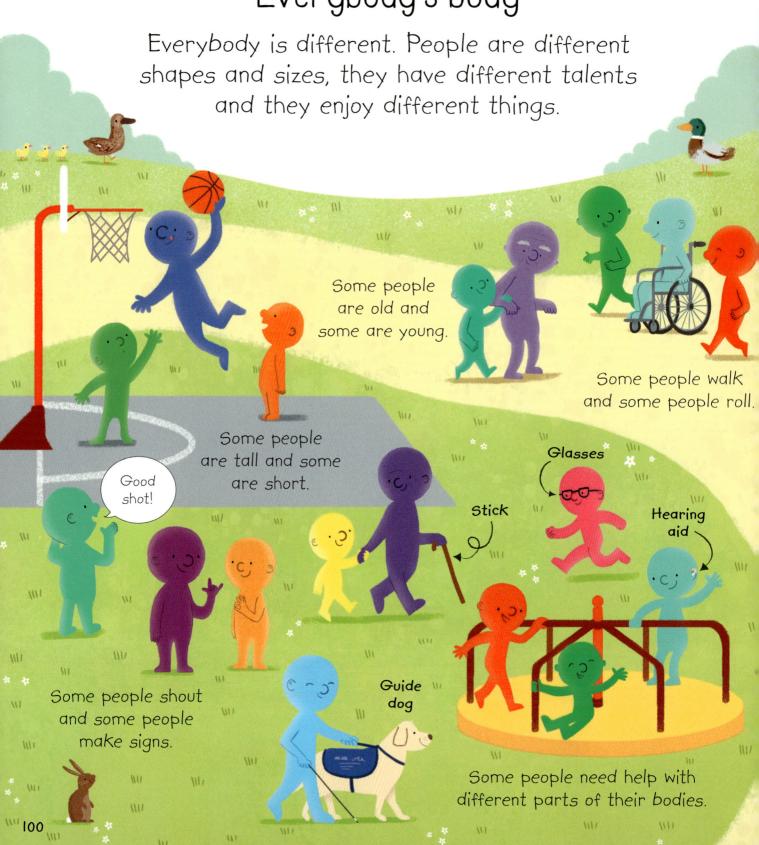

Body parts

Bodies are made from lots of different parts that do different jobs. This is how some of them fit together.

The outside of your body is covered by a layer of skin.

Underneath your skin is a thick layer of stretchy muscles that helps you move.

Under your muscles, there is a hard frame of bones that holds you up. This is your skeleton.

There is a network of blood vessels, too. These are tubes that carry blood to every part of your body.

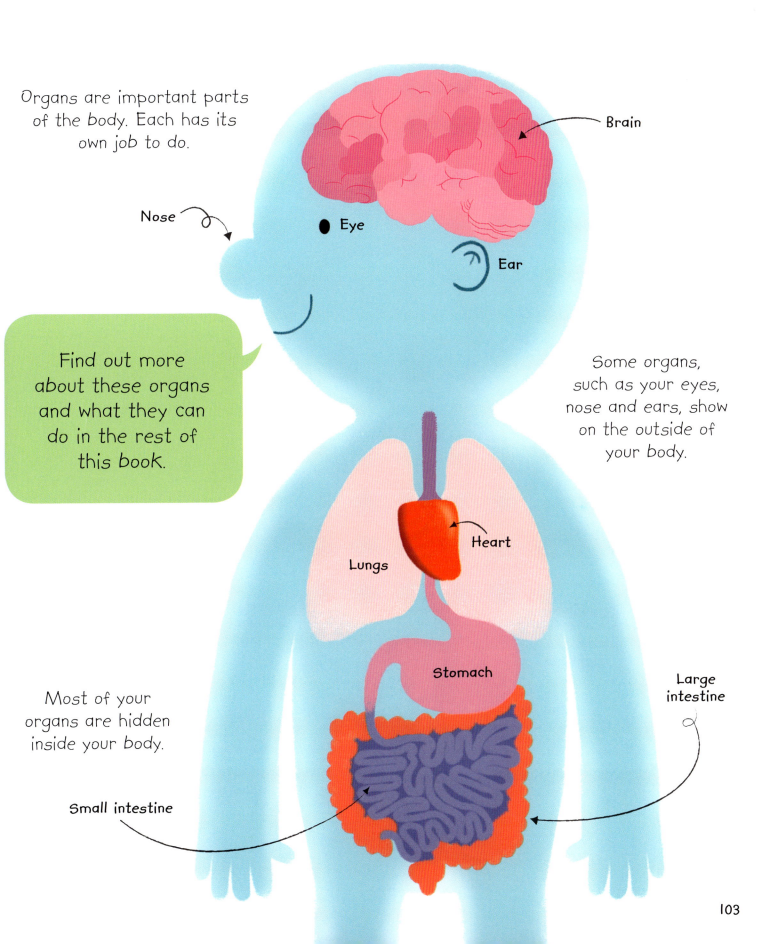

Strong bones

Everyone has hundreds of bones inside their body. Bones are strong and hard and they fit together to make a *skeleton*.

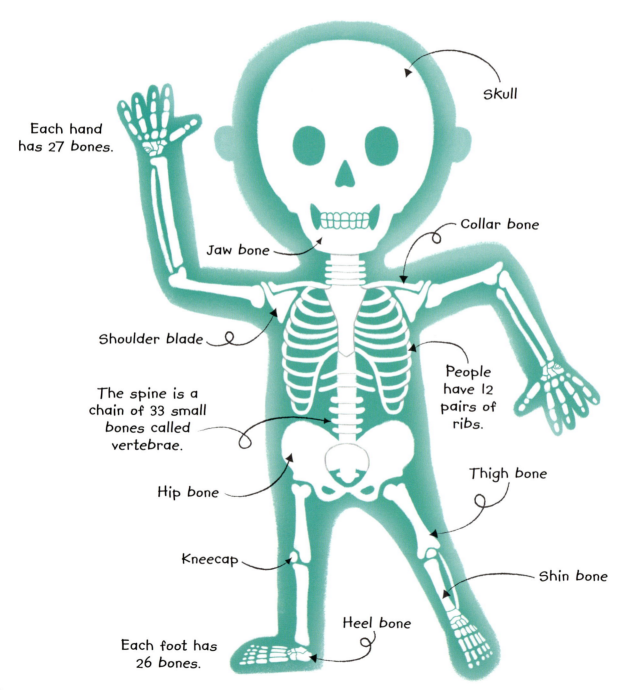

Skull

Each hand has 27 bones.

Jaw bone

Collar bone

Shoulder blade

People have 12 pairs of ribs.

The spine is a chain of 33 small bones called vertebrae.

Hip bone

Thigh bone

Kneecap

Shin bone

Heel bone

Each foot has 26 bones.

People can move their bodies at places called joints, where two bones join together. Different joints move in different ways.

Bones are strong, but sometimes they can break.

Doctors put cases called casts on them to fix them.

The broken bones grow back together in the cast.

Foods like these help your bones grow strong.

You can also keep your bones healthy by playing outside...

and wearing protective gear for sports.

Muscle power

Muscles are strong and stretchy.
They help people move their bodies.

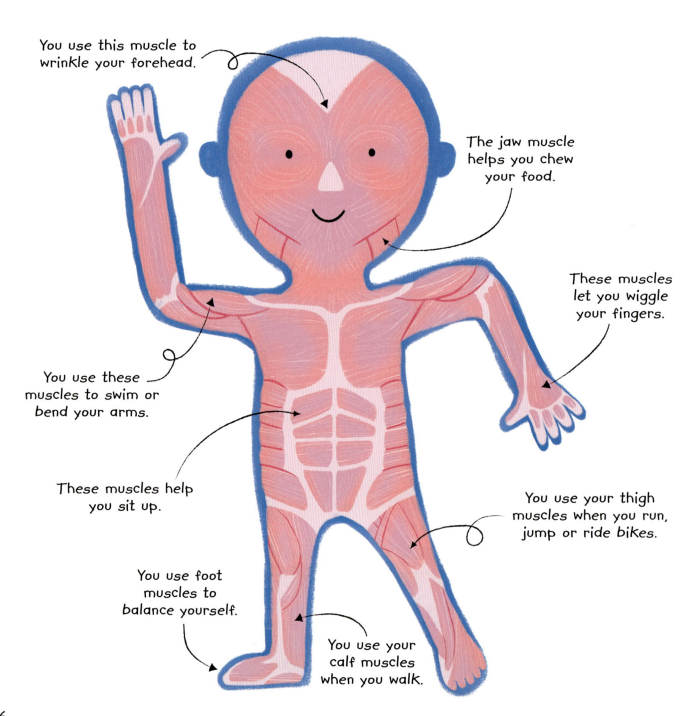

Every time you move your body, you're using muscles.

The more you use your muscles, the stronger they become.

Some muscles work without you thinking about them.
You don't decide to use these muscles, but you can sometimes feel them working.

Sensing the world

There are five main ways that you can *sense* things, by touching, hearing, seeing, smelling and tasting.

The busy brain

Inside everyone's head is an organ called the brain. It controls almost everything that you do, using different areas to do different jobs.

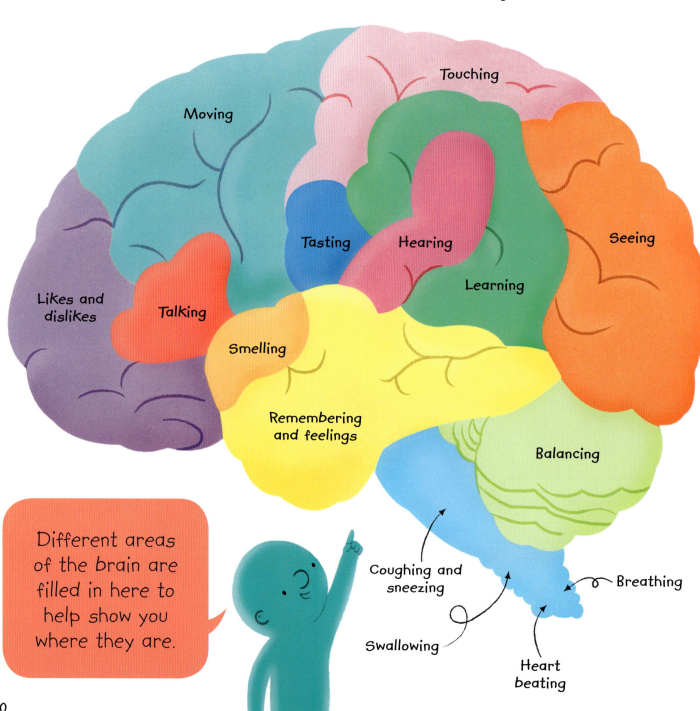

Different areas of the brain are filled in here to help show you where they are.

Your brain recognizes everything that you sense.

Sometimes you know when you're using your brain, such as when you're concentrating or thinking about something.

You also use your brain without realizing it, such as when you blink or breathe. Your brain works all the time to keep you alive.

Eating and drinking

You have to eat food and drink water for your body to work properly. To stay healthy, you need to eat many different types of food.

Everyone needs to be careful not to eat too many sweet, salty or fatty foods.

And everyone needs to drink plenty of water, too.

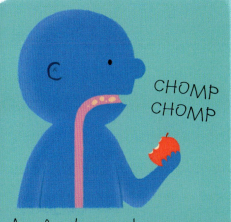

Any food you eat goes on a journey through your body.

CHOMP CHOMP

Muscles squeeze food pipes to move the food along.

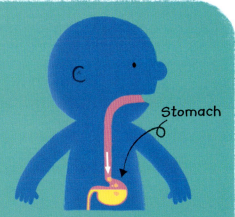

The food passes into your stomach.

In your small intestine, tiny bits of food pass into your blood and give your body energy to work.

Stomach juices mix with the food, and muscles mush it up.

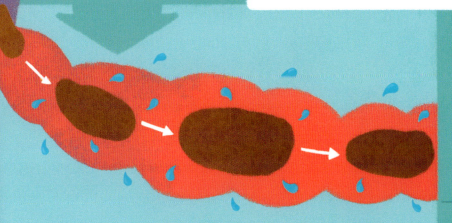

The remaining food moves into your large intestine where water from it passes into your body.

Anything your body doesn't need is pushed out.

Deep breaths

When you breathe air, you take something called oxygen into your body. Everyone needs oxygen to stay alive, so you breathe all the time, even when you're asleep.

People breathe in through their noses and mouths.

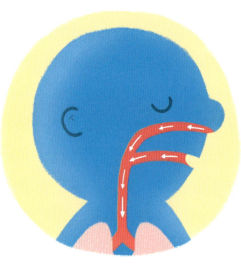

Air travels down a tube known as a windpipe...

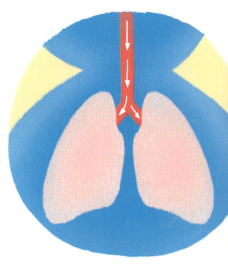

and into a pair of spongy organs called lungs.

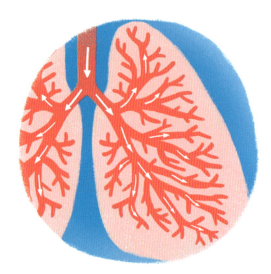

The air travels along smaller and smaller tubes...

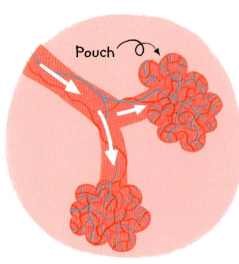

and into tiny pouches...

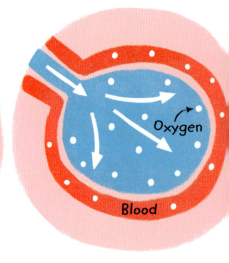

where oxygen from the air passes into the blood.

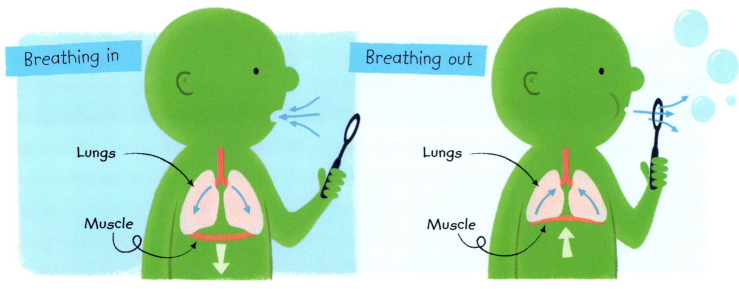

A muscle under your lungs helps you breathe by moving up and down.
It pulls down to fill your lungs with air and it springs back up to empty them.

You breathe out leftover air your body doesn't need.

You cough to clear dirt from your lungs.

You sneeze to clear dirt from your nose.

When people exercise they can become out of breath.
This is because their bodies are working hard and need more oxygen.

Pumping blood

Your heart is an organ that pumps blood to every part of your body. Your heart never stops pumping and your blood never stops moving – it just travels around and around.

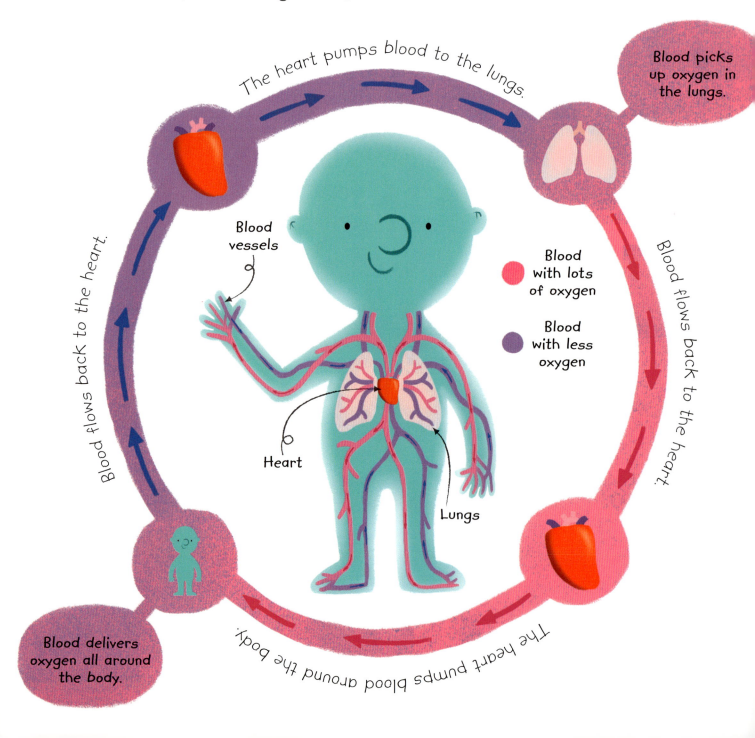

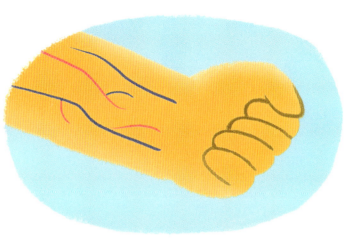

Some blood vessels show through skin. They look like lines.

Doctors can feel your heart pumping blood around your body.

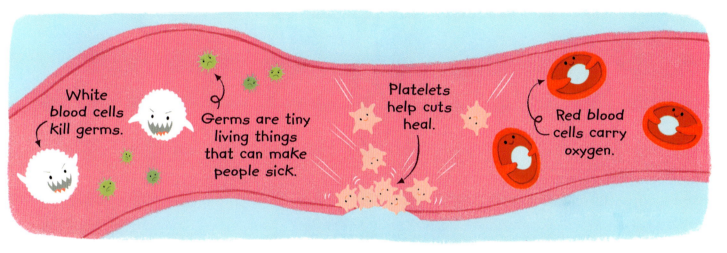

Different things inside blood do different jobs. Some protect the body and some deliver oxygen, food and other things around it.

When a person bleeds, platelets collect near the cut.

This makes the blood sticky, so it dries into a scab.

The scab protects the cut as it heals, then it falls off.

Express yourself

You can use your body to show others what you're thinking and feeling. You can do this by talking, but there are other ways, too.

People use air from their lungs when they talk or sing.

The air wobbles flaps in their throats called vocal cords.

When vocal cords wobble they make sounds come out.

Thank you very much! Thank you!

People use their lips and tongues to turn these sounds into words.

Sleeping at the end of the day gives your body a rest...

so you have more energy and feel fresher when you wake up.

People dream because their brains are still working when they're asleep.

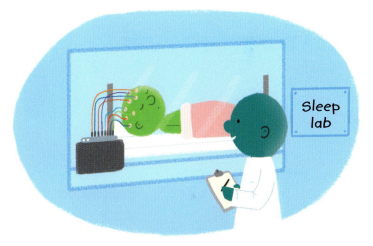
Scientists think sleep helps the brain organize itself and remember things.

When people haven't slept enough they might yawn...

they might start to feel grumpy...

or they might have dark circles under their eyes.

Sickness and health

Most of the time, your body works without a problem, but sometimes it doesn't. When this happens you can start to feel unwell.

When you feel unwell or hurt yourself, you can visit a doctor. The doctor can find out what's wrong and help you get better.

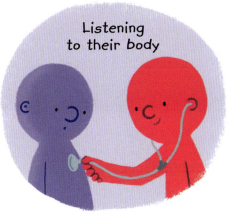

Sometimes doctors can tell what's wrong by checking a person's body from the outside.

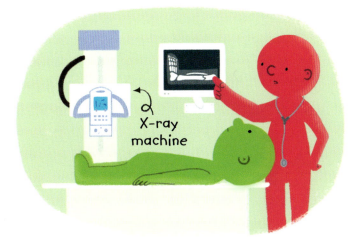

Sometimes they use machines that let them *see* inside the body.

Often they can find out what's wrong just by talking to people.

When doctors know what's wrong, they can help people by giving them medicines or taking care of them in other ways.

123

Taking care of your body

When you take care of your body, you're less likely to be unwell. Here are a few things that you can do every day to keep healthy.

Play sports

Ride a bike

Exercising helps your heart and other parts of your body stay healthy.

Run around

Drink plenty of water

Eat different types of food

You'll be stronger and have more energy if you eat and drink sensibly.

Wash yourself

Brush your teeth

Staying clean will keep germs away and stop you from getting sick.

Get enough sleep

Relax

Your body and your brain need plenty of rest to stay healthy.

Enjoy hobbies

Solve puzzles

Learn new things

Your brain needs exercise, just like your body.

Talk about any problems

Avoid too much screen time

Doing these things will help you feel happier.

Growing up

Early years

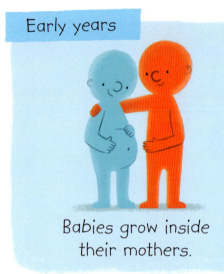
Babies grow inside their mothers.

Newly born babies grow very quickly.

Later their teeth start to come through.

Toddler to teenager

As children get older, they learn to talk.

They have more control of their bodies.

They lose their baby teeth and grow big ones.

Later years

In time, people stop growing and become grown-ups.

Some grown-ups have children.

Sometimes their children go on to have children.

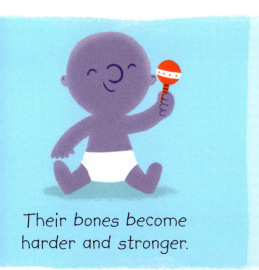
Their bones become harder and stronger.

Their brains grow and develop quickly.

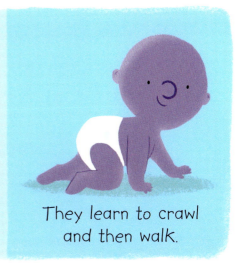
They learn to crawl and then walk.

They become stronger.

Sometimes they grow in sudden bursts.

They grow more hair and might get pimples.

Their hair might go white or they might get wrinkles.

People may become smaller as they get older.

They might need extra help using their bodies.

Your amazing body

Your body is incredibly hard-working and it's busy every second of your life. It's also quicker and stronger than you might realize and full of other surprises, too.

Your bones are stronger than steel.

Messages from your brain can travel around your body faster than a speeding car.

It can take up to 3 days for the food you eat to pass through your body.

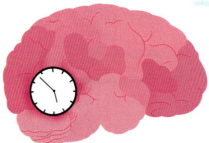

A tiny part of your brain works like a clock and keeps track of the time.

During your life, you will probably end up walking further than 3 times around the world.

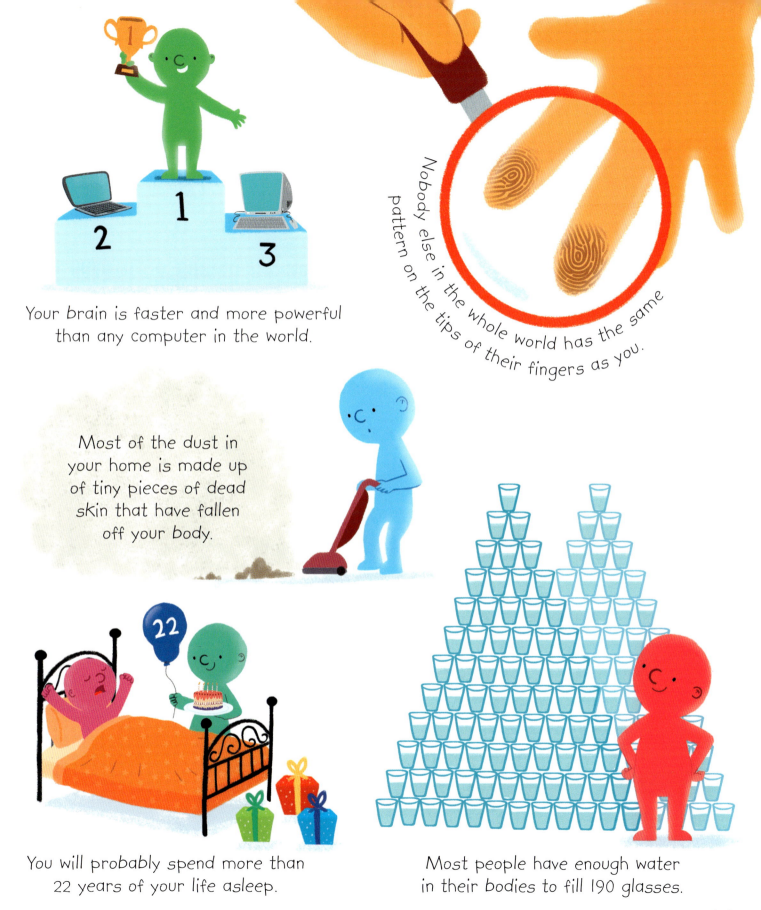

Your brain is faster and more powerful than any computer in the world.

Nobody else in the whole world has the same pattern on the tips of their fingers as you.

Most of the dust in your home is made up of tiny pieces of dead skin that have fallen off your body.

You will probably spend more than 22 years of your life asleep.

Most people have enough water in their bodies to fill 190 glasses.

All sorts of animals

There are millions of different animals living around the world.

Here are some of the animals that live in Africa.

Elephant

Some are very big.

Some are very small.

Dung beetle

Crocodile

SNAP!

Some live on land.

Zebra

Some live in water.

Growing up

Butterfly

A butterfly has laid a tiny egg on this leaf.

Out of the egg comes a caterpillar.

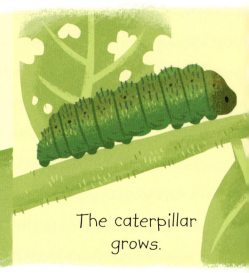
The caterpillar grows.

Penguin

A mother penguin has laid an egg.

Parents keep the egg warm while a chick grows inside.

A chick hatches from the egg.

Gorilla

This gorilla is pregnant – a baby gorilla is growing inside her.

The newborn baby is carried everywhere.

It gets bigger and can play on its own.

It changes into a hard chrysalis.

Inside it turns into a butterfly, then breaks out.

Adult butterfly

The chick's parents bring it food.

When it's big enough to swim on its own, it leaves its parents.

Adult penguin

Older gorillas teach it how to be an adult.

After a few years the gorilla is big, strong and fully grown.

A place to live

Animals need a place to sleep, where they can stay hidden and safe. Many animals build themselves homes to live in and to protect their babies.

This rainforest tree is home to lots of different creatures.

Harpy eagles build nests out of sticks.

Sloths sleep on high branches.

Oriole

Oriole birds weave hanging nests.

A toucan has set up home in the trunk.

Tree frogs live on these big leaves.

Resting jaguar

Sleeping snake

This anteater has dug a hole to rest in.

Leaf-cutter ants' nest

Anteater

137

Finding food

Eating is a big part of an animal's day. Animals have to find, hunt or catch their own food.

Some animals hunt and eat other animals. They are called carnivores.

Hawks hunt smaller birds in mid-air.

Wolves

AWOO!

This wolf is stalking a deer.

Grizzly bear

Salmon

A lynx is looking for a hare to eat.

This hare is staying out of sight.

Duck diving for fish

Wings and feathers

There are thousands of different kinds of birds. They all hatch from eggs, and have feathers, wings and beaks. But they all look and act differently.

Lots of birds live by the sea.

Puffins make nests in the cliffs.

Puffin carrying fish back to its nest

Black-backed gulls

SQUAWK!

This big black-backed gull is snatching food out of a puffin's mouth.

Herring gull

This cormorant is drying out its wings in the sun.

Gannets dive into the water to catch fish.

Woodpeckers tap into trees to find insects to eat.

Swallows sing to each other.

Chickens sit on their eggs to keep them warm.

The bee hummingbird is the smallest bird in the world.

The ostrich is the biggest bird in the world.

Vultures feast on other animals' leftovers.

Flamingos eat pink food. It turns their feathers pink.

Penguins can't fly. They use their wings to swim.

Deadly weapons

Sometimes animals fight to defend themselves, catch food or prove who is the strongest. Sharp teeth or claws can help them win the fight.

Elk fight to see who's toughest.

Antlers

Jagged teeth for biting

Piranha

Elephant

Some snakes can shoot poison through their fangs.

TSSSSSSSss

Tusks

Rattlesnake

Bugs and slugs

There are more creepy crawlies in the world than any other type of animal. They're small, but there are millions of them.

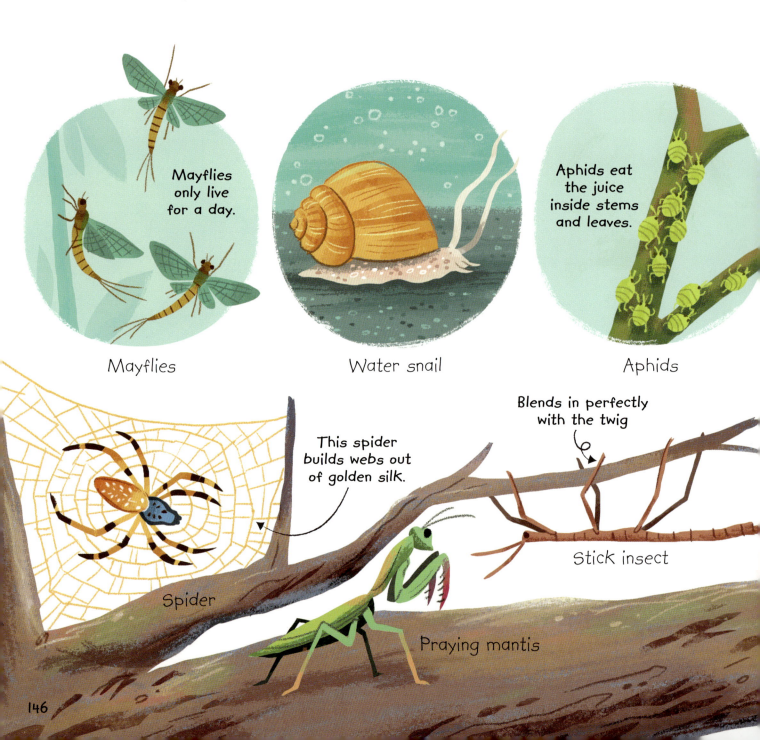

Mayflies only live for a day.

Mayflies

Water snail

Aphids eat the juice inside stems and leaves.

Aphids

This spider builds webs out of golden silk.

Spider

Blends in perfectly with the twig

Stick insect

Praying mantis

Hot and cold

Some animals live in places where it's baking hot or freezing cold.

Camels store fat in their humps. They turn it into energy when they can't find food.

This gazelle has found some grass to eat.

Scorpion

Dung beetles

Lizards

Sand foxes

This viper has horns that might stop sand from getting in its eyes.

This is a hot, dry desert. There's not much water and hardly any plants. Most of the animals here are pale, to blend in with the sand.

This is the frozen Arctic. Not much can live here and not much grows. Everything is white with snow and ice. Most of the animals are white too, to blend in.

Patterns

Lots of animals are bright and beautiful, with spotted fur, striped skin or flashy feathers, to help them hide or stand out.

Chameleons can turn their skin green to blend in with leaves.

This jellyfish is see-through, to disguise it in the ocean.

Leopards are the same shade as the grass they skulk in.

Fancy patterns stand out from the crowd.
They say, "Look at me!"

A peacock's tail helps him impress females.

Peacock

Birds of paradise

Bright cheeks

Chameleons completely change how they look, to show off.

Mandrill

Bright stripes or spots can mean,
"Don't eat me - I'm dangerous!"

Vivid blue skin

Poison dart frog

Wasp

Salamander

Yellow and black animals are often poisonous.

Warning stripes

Coral snake

Monarch caterpillar

The deer with the loudest roar takes charge.

Praying mantises spread their legs to look bigger and scare off other animals.

Skunks spray a smelly liquid to tell attackers not to come closer.

Pufferfish puff out their stomachs to warn bigger fish they'd be hard to eat.

In the dark

Some animals spend most of their lives in the dark, some under the sea, some only coming out at night.

Light from the sun doesn't reach the deepest parts of the ocean.
The deeper you go, the harder it is to live.

Some animals sleep during the day and come out when the sun sets and it gets dark.

Bats

Fireflies

Moths

Barn owl chicks

Barn owl

TWIT TWOO!

Sleeping bat

Foxes

Wood mouse

Hedgehog

Animals that come out at night are called nocturnal animals.

CROAK

Toad catching insects

Otter

Night animals have good noses and ears so they can find their way around in the dark.

Animal journeys

Animals are always on the move, but some go on amazingly long journeys. They travel across the planet each year to find food, sunshine, or to lay their eggs.

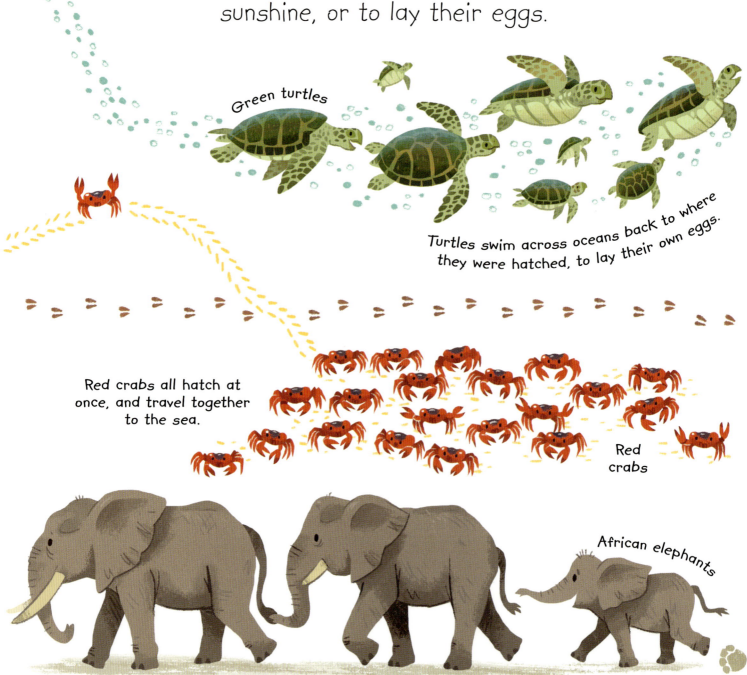

Green turtles

Turtles swim across oceans back to where they were hatched, to lay their own eggs.

Red crabs all hatch at once, and travel together to the sea.

Red crabs

African elephants

Elephants walk miles and miles every day to find enough food to fill them up.

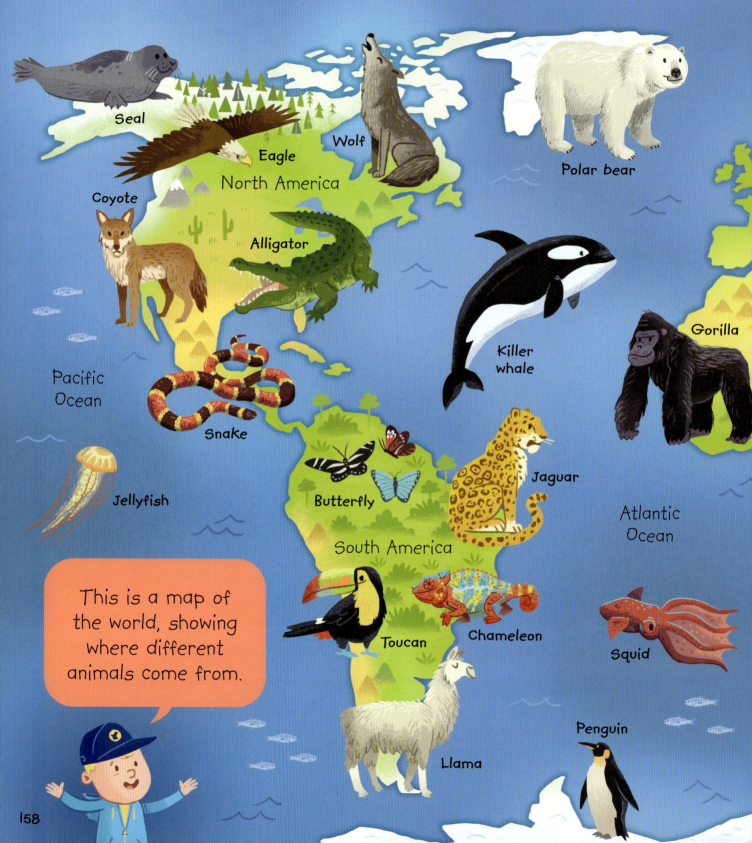

Dinosaurs

Big and small

Dinosaurs were the largest animals that have ever walked on land. Nobody knows which type was the very biggest, because people keep finding bigger bones.

Some dinosaurs were rather small. The smallest we know of were around the size of a duck.

Human being

Microraptor

Minmi

Citipati

Protoceratops

Ankylosaurus

Microceratus

Compsognathus

This tail alone was the same length as a python.

These legs were twice the height of an adult human.

Where did dinosaurs come from?

Dinosaurs weren't the first animals that lived on the Earth. Before them, came crawling animals – and even before them, there were swimming animals in the sea.

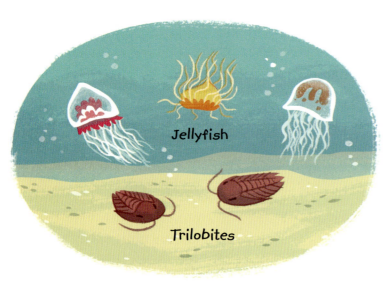

The very first animals swam or floated under water. They had no arms or legs.

Fish with flippers were the first creatures to crawl out of the water.

Some of the first animals that lived on land were scaly creatures a little like dinosaurs. Their legs stuck out on either side, and they crawled with their bellies close to the ground.

Inside a dinosaur

No one really knows what any dinosaur looked like on the outside. But we know a lot about their bones, and some other inside parts, too.

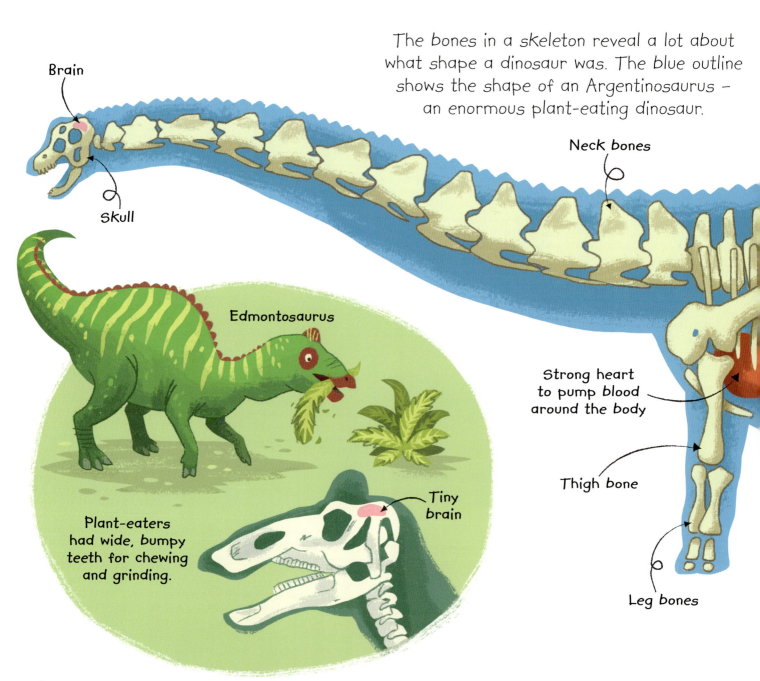

The bones in a skeleton reveal a lot about what shape a dinosaur was. The blue outline shows the shape of an Argentinosaurus – an enormous plant-eating dinosaur.

Plant-eating dinosaurs chewed their food very thoroughly.

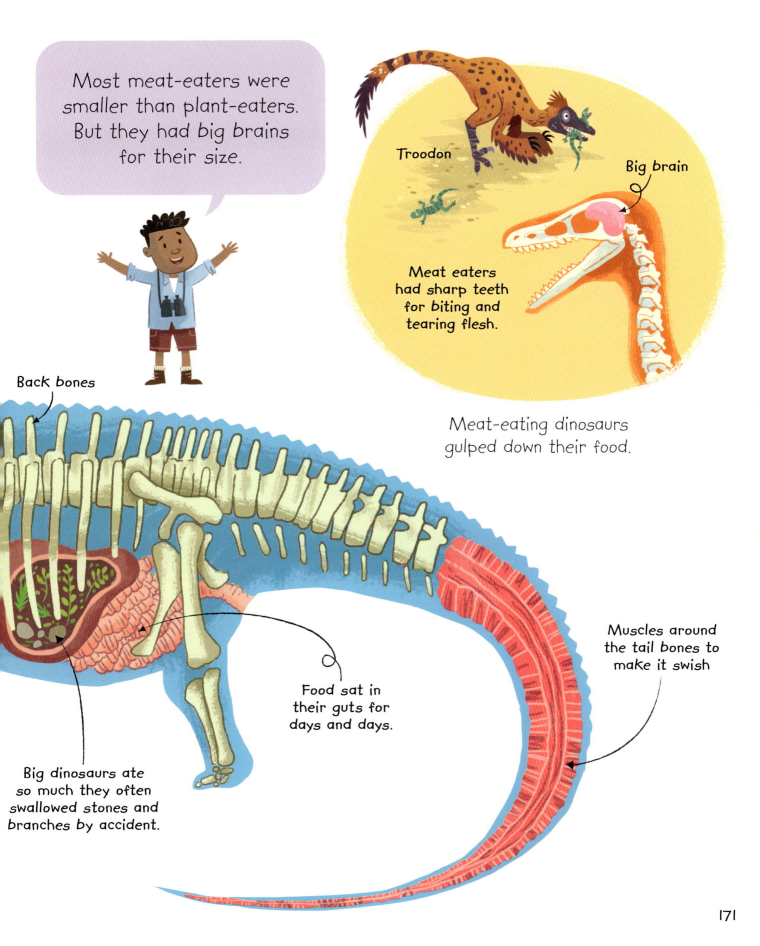

Growing up

All dinosaurs, big and small, hatched from eggs. Even the largest dinosaurs laid eggs that were no bigger than a football.

A mother Citipati has just laid a clutch of eggs.

The father sits on the nest to keep the eggs warm.

Inside each egg, a tiny baby Citipati grows.

After a few weeks, the eggs are ready to hatch.

The babies peck their way out from inside.

The parents bring food for the children.

Under the sea

In the time of the dinosaurs, massive creatures with big teeth prowled the oceans.

What happened to the dinosaurs?

Many millions of years ago, a huge disaster killed off all kinds of animals, including dinosaurs. Scientists are still trying to learn exactly how it happened.

It all began when an enormous rock from space came crashing into planet Earth...

...the rock made a hole in a place called Yucatan, on the east coast of Mexico.

Alamosaurus

Tyrannosaurus

Edmontosaurus

Triceratops

Tylosaurus

The crashing rock set off many earthquakes and tsunamis.

Huge clouds of dust filled the sky.

The dust spread out and covered the Earth.

It grew cold and dark, and many plants died out...

...so all the plant-eating dinosaurs died out, too.

And, in time, so did the meat-eaters.

But a few small animals survived. These included furry mammals, and feathered dinosaurs – now called birds.

Bones and fossils

Dinosaur hunters are called paleontologists. They dig into the ground to find the remains of long-dead dinosaurs.

Millions of years ago...

A dinosaur dies and its body is covered in mud.

Its body rots away, leaving only a skeleton.

Hundreds of years later, it's buried under layers of rocks

When it rains, water trickles into the bones.

Chemicals in the water react with the bones...

...and slowly turn them into fossils.

Millions of years later...

Rain and wind wear away the rocks and the fossils.

A few fossils end up near the surface of the soil...

...where a fossil hunter can find them.

Paleontologists dig up the fossils very carefully.

Then they scrape all the dirt off.

Often, many fossil bones are missing.

Paleontologists make new bones to fill in any missing pieces.

Paleontologists have to work out how all the bones fit together.

The changing world of dinosaurs

Dinosaurs didn't all live at the same time. Over the years, they appeared in many different shapes and sizes, too.

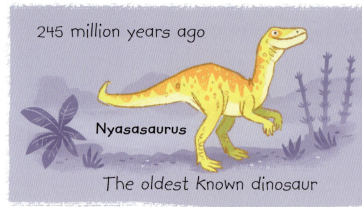

245 million years ago
Nyasasaurus
The oldest known dinosaur

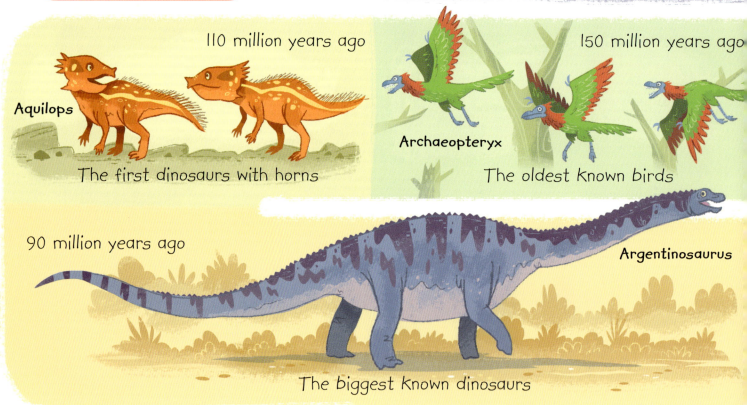

110 million years ago
Aquilops
The first dinosaurs with horns

150 million years ago
Archaeopteryx
The oldest known birds

90 million years ago
Argentinosaurus
The biggest known dinosaurs

Timeline of animals

The first ever animals

500 million years ago

The first fish

The first insects
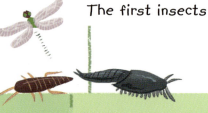
400 million years ago

The first reptiles
300 million years ago

10,000 years ago

The Stone Age

Thousands of years ago, people didn't live in houses or grow food on farms. They moved from place to place, looking for food in the wild.

This time is called the Stone Age because people made tools from stones, and sometimes deer antlers, bone and wood too.

After a while, some Stone-Age people found out how to grow their own food. They started to build houses and settle in one place.

Later still, people learned to make strong, sharp tools from a metal called bronze and ornaments from gold. This time is called the Bronze Age.

3,500 years ago

The Pharaoh's land

People now known as the Ancient Egyptians lived along the River Nile in North Africa. Here they built magnificent temples and tombs called pyramids.

Most of Ancient Egypt was a dusty desert, but the River Nile flowed through the whole country, carrying boats and bringing water to grow food.

Ancient Egypt was ruled by a powerful king called a pharaoh.

Spells written in a picture writing called hieroglyphics

Stone headrest to sleep on (instead of a pillow)

Perfumes

Golden furniture

Clothes

Solid gold coffin

Jewels

Games

Preserved food

The Ancient Egyptians believed in a life after death, so they buried their pharaohs with things for them to use after they died.

2,500 years ago

The Iron Age

A time known as the Iron Age began in Europe, when people learned to make things from a strong metal called iron.

People looked for rocks called iron ore.

They heated iron ore in a very hot oven to make iron.

The iron could be hammered into any shape.

Iron-Age people lived and worked together in groups called tribes.

Tribes built tall fences and steep banks around their homes to keep out enemies.

Every tribe had a chief who made decisions and led them into battle.

Priests called druids performed religious ceremonies.

Warriors were trained to use weapons to defend the tribe.

A bard told stories and sang songs about the tribe's great leaders.

Most Iron-Age people worked as farmers.

Craftworkers made things from iron, wood and clay.

2,000 years ago

Roving Romans

The Romans were people from the city of Rome in Italy. Their army conquered vast amounts of land where they built new cities, and roads linking them together.

Shield

Crested helmet

Sword

Scabbard (sword holder)

Dagger

Javelin for throwing

Breastplate

Protective apron

Tunic

Sandals

These things are a Roman soldier's battle gear.

1,400 years ago

Tang China

At this time, China was ruled by a family of emperors called the Tang. Under the Tang, the country became peaceful and rich.

Over a million people lived in the Tang city of Chang'an. There were many majestic palaces and towers called pagodas inside the city walls.

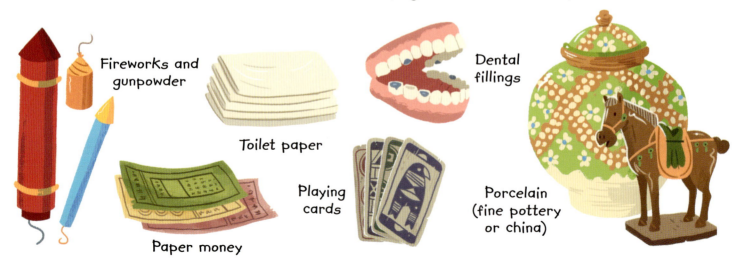

Lots of inventions made by people from the Tang dynasty are still used today.

Tang emperors set a difficult exam to find the cleverest people to help them run the country. The exam covered lots of subjects.

Archery

Law

Mathematics

Music

Fighting

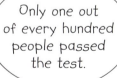

Poetry

Only one out of every hundred people passed the test.

1,200 years ago

Mighty Maya

The Maya were people who lived in Central America. They cleared large areas of jungle to build several big cities, each with its own king.

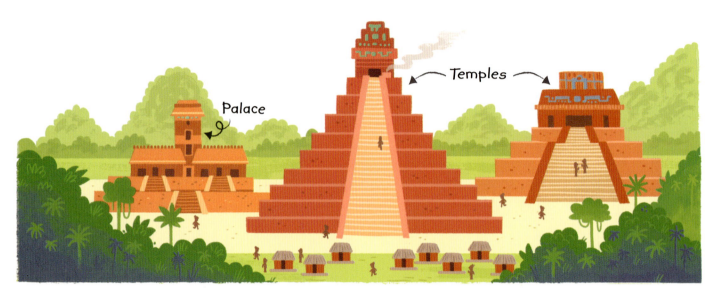

Every Maya city had a palace, where the king lived, and stone temples, where some kings were buried and astronomers studied the stars.

Important cities also had a ball court for a game called *Pok a Tok*. The Maya didn't just play this game for fun, it was also part of their religion.

The Maya invented a way of writing using symbols, called glyphs, which stood for different words or sounds.

Most ordinary Maya worked as farmers, growing food to feed people in the city.

The Maya didn't have money. They exchanged goods with each other, or they paid with feathers, cocoa or objects made from valuable materials such as gold.

1,000 years ago

Sailors and raiders

People called Vikings lived in Northern Europe. They were famous for being fierce warriors, but they were also farmers, craftworkers and excellent sailors.

When good farming land ran out, the Vikings looked for new opportunities.

Some made their living away from farms, learning new crafts.

Some went to live in other parts of Europe and even reached North America.

Meanwhile, Viking traders roamed as far away as Baghdad in Iraq.

Before Vikings settled in new places, they often attacked or raided local towns and villages, taking people prisoner and stealing their treasure.

800 years ago

Castle town

Hundreds of years ago, people all over Europe were fighting wars with each other. To keep safe, kings and lords built strong castles and, later on, tall walls around towns.

600 years ago

City of mud

Adventurous traders risked their lives to reach Timbuktu in West Africa. The city became famous for its universities, libraries and great wealth.

Timbuktu grew up where the sandy Sahara desert met the River Niger.

Gold-seeking traders rested here after dangerous desert journeys.

The traders set up a market where they swapped goods and slaves with each other.

The traders grew rich, building grand houses and city walls from mud bricks.

In Timbuktu's busy markets, people could buy salt from the north, gold from the south and books from the east.

The traders spread the Muslim faith and brought scholars with them who set up one of the world's first universities in Timbuktu.

400 years ago

Buzzing London

London in England was an exciting, crowded city. It grew bigger and bigger as people moved from the country, hoping to make their fortune.

During especially cold winters, the River Thames froze solid. Frost fairs were held on the ice, where people would skate, set up stalls and play games.

Ships brought goods from all over the world to London's busy port.

Some people were very poor. They were forced to steal and beg to make a living.

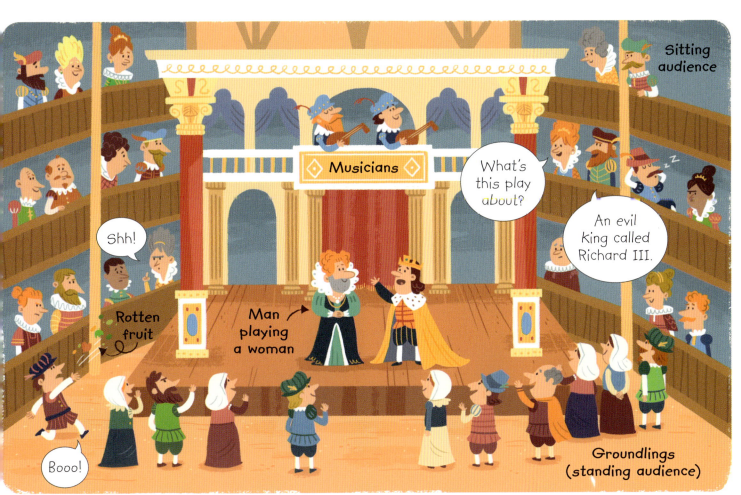

Famous writers, such as William Shakespeare, wrote plays that were performed in playhouses in front of a crowd that could be loud and rowdy.

Old Japan

300 years ago

Edo (the old name for Tokyo) in Japan was the largest city in the world. This time in Japanese history is known as the Edo period.

During the Edo period, Japan had emperors, but they didn't have any power. Instead, leaders called shoguns ruled the country from a castle in Edo.

Edo people loved nature. They grew beautiful gardens and arranged flowers.

They drank tea together to relax, as part of a ceremony with strict rules.

Soldiers known as samurai wore fierce-looking clothes for fighting. This was mostly for show, because the Edo period was so peaceful.

In their free time, people watched shows called kabuki plays. Actors wore elaborate make-up and danced to music.

The Gold Rush

170 years ago

The Gold Rush was a time when people from all over the world hurried to California in North America, hoping to find gold.

The first people in California were Native Americans.

Thousands of years later, Europeans arrived.

Later still, two men found gold in the area.

The news spread all around the world.

Thousands of people set off to find gold, but there were no maps, so trail guides showed the way.

"You'll be safe if you follow me."

At first, miners found gold in river water.

Then they started to dig for it underground.

The miners forced the Native Americans to leave.

Sometimes there were fights over land.

Only a few miners found their fortune in the gold mines, but local traders grew very rich.

After a while, gold became harder to find.

Many miners went home empty handed.

Some chose to stay and farm the land.

How do we know about long ago?

You can learn about life in the past by visiting museums and old buildings. Here you can find treasures that people have saved from long ago.

Edo costume (300 years ago)

Native American costume (170 years ago)

Painting of London (400 years ago)

Knight costume (800 years ago)

Some art shows how people and places used to look long ago.

Tang pottery (1,400 years ago)

Roman statue (2,000 years ago)

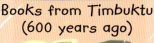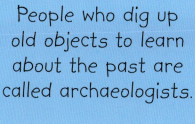

Where and when?

These pages haven't only taken you on a journey through time, they've also taken you on a trip around the world. Look back through the pages to see who lived where – as well as when.

Stone-Age hunter
Europe
10,000 years ago

You can use this map to see where each of the characters on the next page lived.

Ancient Egyptian musician
Africa
3,500 years ago

Iron-Age farmer
Europe
2,500 years ago

Roman soldier
Europe
2,000 years ago

Tang poet
Asia
1,400 years ago

Maya ball player
North America
1,200 years ago

Viking warrior
Europe
1,000 years ago

Castle Knight
Europe
800 years ago

Timbuktu trader
Africa
600 years ago

London lady
Europe
400 years ago

Edo woman
Asia
300 years ago

Gold Rush miner
North America
170 years ago

Factory worker
Europe
130 years ago

Index

A

Aerodactylus, 174
Africa, 188-189, 202-203, 214, 215
air, 44, 80-81, 85, 88, 101, 114, 115
Alamosaurus, 178
alligators, 158
Allosaurus, 164
ammonites, 177
anemones, 144, 145
animals, 8, 9, 12, 14, 15, 16, 17, 18, 19, 21, 22, 23, 24, 25, 26, 27, 29, 130-161, 165, 168, 169, 182,
Ankylosaurus, 166
anteaters, 137
antelopes, 133
ants, 137
Anurognathus, 174
Apatosaurus, 164
aqueducts, 193
Archaeopteryx, 175, 182
Argentinosaurus, 170-171, 182

Asia, 194-195, 206-207, 214, 215
Asteroid Belt, 57
asteroids, 43, 56, 57
astronauts, 41, 45, 46-47, 48, 49, 50, 51, 52, 53, 54, 55, 67
astronomers, 40, 196
atmosphere, 43
Australasia, 214
axes, 186, 187, 213

B

babies, 126, 127, 172-173
Baghdad, 198
bats, 15, 29, 155
bears, 136, 138, 149, 158
beavers, 139
bees, 93, 136, 143
beetles, 147, 161
Big Dipper, 69
binoculars, 66

birds, 9, 14, 15, 17, 18, 19, 21, 23, 25, 136, 137, 138, 140-141, 149, 151, 152, 155, 157, 158, 159, 160, 179, 183
blizzards, 34
blood, 102, 107, 113, 114, 116-117
body, 74, 96, 98-129
bones, 102, 104, 127, 128, 170-171, 180-181
books, 203, 213
Brachiosaurus, 165
brain, 103, 110-111, 121, 125, 127, 128, 129, 170-171
breathing, 80, 110, 111, 114-115, 120
Britain, 210-211
Bronze Age, 187
butterflies, 134, 135, 147, 157, 158

C

California, 208
Callipterus, 176
Camarasaurus, 164
camels, 14, 15, 148, 159
cardboard, 83
castles, 200-201, 206, 215
caterpillars, 134, 135, 139, 151
caves, 25, 29
cells, 101, 117
Central America, 196-197
Ceratosaurus, 165
chameleons, 150, 151, 158
Chang'an, 194
changing, 86-87
cheetahs, 133, 161
China, 194-195
cities, 8, 23, 33, 35, 192, 196, 197, 202, 204
Citipati, 166, 172
clay, 84
coasts, 24-25
Coelacanth, 176
Coelophysis, 183
comets, 43, 57
Compsognathus, 166
concrete, 82
Confuciusornis, 175
constellations, 69
cooling, 87
coral, 26, 144, 145, 159
coyotes, 153, 158
crabs, 156
craftworkers, 191, 198
crocodiles, 132
crops, 8, 12, 31, 33, 36
cuttlefish, 144

D

dark, 76-77
day, 10, 11
deer, 19, 139, 153, 159
deserts, 10, 14-15, 188, 202
Dimetrodon, 168
dinosaurs, 162-183
Diplodocus, 167
doctors, 122-123
dolphins, 152
dreaming, 120-121
drinking, 112-113
druids, 191

E

ducks, 138
dung beetles, 132, 148, 159, 161

eagles, 133, 137, 158
ears, 103, 108
Earth, 10-11, 13, 14, 20, 26, 36, 42, 43, 44, 51, 53, 55, 56, 67
earthquakes, 32-33
eating, 112-113
Edmontosaurus, 170, 178
Edo, 206-207, 212, 215
eggs, 172, 173
Egypt, 188-189, 213, 215
Elasmosaurus, 177
elastic, 83
electricity, 28, 35, 37, 76
elephants, 132, 142, 156
elk, 142
emperors, 195, 206
energy, 113, 121
England, 204
Eoraptor, 169

217

equator, 13
Eryops, 168
Eudimorphodon, 183
Europe, 190-191, 192-193, 198-199, 200-201, 204-205, 210-211, 214, 215
Exaeretodon, 169
Excalibosaurus, 176
exercise, 115, 124, 125
experiments, 74, 75, 85, 96-97
eyes, 103, 109

F

fabric, 82, 83,
factories, 210-211, 215
falcons, 143, 161
falling, 81
farmers, 191, 197, 200, 209
farms, 8, 36
feathers, 82

feelings, 110, 111, 118
fish, 22, 24, 26, 27, 36, 112, 138, 140 142, 144, 145, 153, 154, 159, 168, 182
fishing, 27, 186
flamingos, 133, 141, 160
floating, 80
flowers, 89, 92-93
flying, 165, 174-175
food, 14, 27, 36, 101, 105, 112, 113, 124, 128
forces, 94-95
forests, 9, 10, 16-17
forum, 193
fossils, 180-181
foxes, 148, 149, 155
Fruitafossor, 165
fruits, 89, 91, 93

G

galaxies, 42, 64-65, 66, 67
Gargoyleosaurus, 164
gazelles, 148
geckos, 153
geese, 157

giraffes, 133, 159
glass, 83, 84
Gnathosaurus, 174
gold, 187, 197, 202, 203, 208, 209, 215
Goniopholis, 165
gorillas, 134, 135, 158
gravity, 95
Great Dog, 69
growing, 97

H

hair, 127
hares, 138, 149
Hatzegopteryx, 175
hearing, 108, 110, 111
heart, 96, 103, 107, 110, 111, 116, 117, 124, 170
heating, 87
hedgehogs, 155
Herrerasaurus, 169
Hubble Space Telescope, 66, 67
hunting, 186, 187
hurricanes, 35

I

ice, 18, 19, 20
Ichthyosaurus, 176
insects, 9, 16, 17, 21, 29, 182
International Space Station, 50-55, 69
intestines, 103, 113
Iraq, 198
Iron Age, 190-191, 213, 215
Ischigualastia, 169
islands, 31
Italy, 192

J

jaguars, 137, 158
Japan, 206-207
jellyfish, 150, 158, 168
joints, 105
jungles, 196
Jupiter, 57

K

Kings, 196, 200
Knights, 201, 215

L

lakes, 20, 23, 36
land, 18, 24, 35
lava, 30-31
learning, 110, 111
leaves, 82, 88, 89, 90-91
leopards, 150
libraries, 202
light, 76-77, 88
lightning, 35
lions, 143
lips, 118
listening, 123
lizards, 148, 164
llamas, 158
lobsters, 143
London, 204-205, 215

long ago, 184-215
longships, 199
looking, 123
lunar module, 45
lungs, 103, 114, 115
lynx, 138

M

Macroplata, 176
magnets, 74, 95
magnifying glass, 75
Maiasaurus, 173
maps, 158-159, 214
markets, 200, 202, 203

219

Mars, 56, 58-59
materials, 82-83, 86-87
Maya, 196-197, 213, 215
medicine, 123
Mercury, 56
metal, 82, 84
mice, 155
Microceratus, 166
Microraptor, 166
microscopes, 75
Milky Way, 65
Minmi, 166
mixing, 86, 87, 96
monkeys, 151, 159, 160
Moon, the, 41, 44-45, 56, 70-71
moons, 42, 56, 57
moose, 139
Mosasaurus, 177
moths, 155
mountains, 8, 9, 10, 20-21, 31
mouths, 114
moving, 94-95, 110
muscles, 102, 106-107, 113, 115, 120, 171
museums, 212
Mussaurus, 169

N

Native Americans, 208, 209, 212
nebulas, 62
nectar, 93
Neptune, 57
Niger river, 202
night, 11
Nile river, 188
North America, 198, 208-209, 214, 215
North Pole, 10, 19
noses, 103, 109, 114
Nyasasaurus, 182

O

oasis, 14
oceans, 8, 10, 23, 24-25, 26-27, 31, 33, 36, 176-177
orangutans, 136, 159

organs, 103, 107, 114, 116
Orion the Hunter, 69
Ornitholestes, 164
Ornithomimus, 173, 183
ostriches, 133, 141
Othnielosaurus, 164
otters, 155, 159
our world, 6-37
owls, 15, 149, 155
oxygen, 115, 116, 117

P

pagoda, 194
palaces, 194, 196
pandas, 159
paper, 84
penguins, 18, 134, 135, 141, 158
people, 8, 9, 14, 18, 19, 21, 25, 27
pharaohs, 188, 189
planets, 42, 56, 57, 66, 69
plants, 8, 12, 15, 16, 17, 20, 21, 24, 88-89, 90-91, 92-93, 97

plastic, 82-83
Platecarpus, 177
Plateosaurus, 183
plays, 205, 207
Plesiosaurus, 176
Pluto, 57
pollen, 93
praying mantis, 146, 153
priests, 189, 191
Protoceratops, 166
Pterodactylus, 174
pterosaurs, 174-175
pulling, 95
pushing, 94
pyramids, 188

Q

Quetzalcoatlus, 175

R

rabbits, 136
rain, 13, 22
rainbow, 77
rainforests, 16-17
reflections, 77
Rhamphorhynchus, 174
rhinos, 143
Rhomaleosaurus, 176
Riojasaurus, 169
rivers, 9, 17, 22-23, 29, 35, 36, 188, 202, 204, 209
roads, 192, 193
rockets, 41, 43, 48-49
rocks, 20, 24, 25, 29, 30, 31, 82
Romans, 192-193, 212, 215
Rome, 192
roots, 88, 89
rovers, 58-59
rubber, 83
rulers, 75

S

salamander, 151
samurai, 207
sand, 14-15, 34, 35, 36, 148
satellites, 43
Saturn, 57
scabs, 117
Scaphognathus, 165, 174
science, 72-97
scientists, 74, 75, 121
scorpions, 143, 148, 159
seahorses, 145
seals, 18, 149, 158
seas, 8, 10, 18, 19, 23, 24-25, 26-27, 31, 33, 35, 36, 176-177
seasons, 12-13, 21
seeds, 91, 93
seeing, 108, 109, 110, 111
senses, 108-109, 111
shadows, 77
sharks, 143, 145, 153, 154, 159, 176
Shastasaurus, 183
shoguns, 206
shooting stars, 69
sickness, 122-123

221

skeletons, 102, 104, 170-171, 180, 181
skin, 102, 129
sleeping, 120-121, 129
sloths, 137
smelling, 108, 109, 110, 111
snakes, 133, 137, 142, 148, 158
snow, 18, 19, 20, 21, 22, 34
soil, 14, 29, 31
Solar System, 56-57
soldiers, 192, 193, 207
sounds, 78-79, 97
South America, 214
South Pole, 18
Soyuz, 48, 49, 50
space, 38-71
space agency, 41
space probes, 43, 66
spacecraft, 41, 46, 47, 48, 49, 50-51, 53, 58, 67

spacesuits, 45, 54, 55
spacewalks, 51, 54-55
spiders, 143, 146, 159
Spinosaurus, 167
sponges, 83
squids, 154, 158, 177
squirrels, 139
starfish, 24, 145
stars, 40, 42, 60-63, 64, 65, 66, 68, 76
Staurikosaurus, 169
steam engines, 210, 211
Stegosaurus, 167
Stenopterygius, 176
Stokesosaurus, 164
stomach, 103, 107, 113
Stone Age, 186-187, 213, 214
stones, 20, 29, 30, 31, 36, 82
stopwatch, 75
storms, 9, 10, 34-35
Sun, the, 11, 14, 37, 40, 56, 60, 61, 65, 68, 76, 77, 92
supernova, 63
swimming, 176-177

T

talking, 111, 118, 126
Tang, 194-195, 212, 215
tasting, 108, 109, 110, 111
teeth, 126, 170-171, 177
telescopes, 40, 66-67
temples, 188, 196
termites, 136
Thames river, 204
thinking, 111, 118
thunder, 35
tigers, 143, 159
Tiktaalik, 168
Timbuktu, 202-203, 213, 215
toads, 155
Tokyo, 206-207
tongues, 109, 118
tornadoes, 34
toucans, 137, 158
touching, 108, 110, 111
towns, 8, 23, 33, 35, 192, 196, 197, 202, 204
traders, 202-203, 209, 215
trees, 16, 17, 20, 29, 33, 35, 36, 88, 89, 90-91, 92
Triceratops, 167, 178

Trilobites, 168
Troodon, 171
tsunamis, 33, 179
turtles, 144, 156, 159
Tylosaurus, 177, 178
typhoons, 35
tyrannosaurs, 167, 178
Tyrannosaurus rex, 167

U

underground, 28-29
universities, 202, 203
Uranus, 57
urchins, 145

V

valley, 22
Venus, 56
Vikings, 198-199, 213, 215

vocal cords, 118
Volaticotherium, 165
volcanoes, 30-31
voles, 139

W

walrus, 143, 159
warriors, 191, 198
water, 13, 14, 15, 19, 21, 23, 24, 25, 26, 27, 28, 31, 35, 36, 37, 77, 83, 88, 95, 101, 124, 129
waves, 24, 25, 33
weather, 12, 13, 20, 34-35
whales, 149, 157, 158, 159, 160-161
wildebeest, 157
wind, 25, 34, 35, 37, 80, 95
wire, 83
wolves, 138, 158, 160
wood, 83
writing, 189, 197

X

x-rays, 123

Z

zebra, 132

Usborne Quicklinks

The internet is a great place for discovering more about the topics in this book. For links to carefully selected websites for young children, go to **usborne.com/Quicklinks** and type in the title of this book.

You'll find links to websites where you can...

...visit the North Pole and see how animals keep warm
...see where an astronaut sleeps on the International Space Station
...watch a video about forces that make things move
...take a peek at your brain and other organs
...find out about the biggest animal on Earth, the blue whale

...and much, much more.

Notes for grown-ups

Please read the internet safety guidelines at Usborne Quicklinks with your child. Children should be supervised online. The websites are regularly reviewed and the links at Usborne Quicklinks are updated. However, Usborne Publishing is not responsible and does not accept liability for the content or availability of any website other than its own.

Expert advisors: Penny Coltman, Dr. Owen Lewis, Dr. Anne Millard,
Dr. Darren Naish, Zoë Simmons, John & Margaret Rostron, Dr. Roger Trend

Managing designer: Nicola Butler

Edited by: Ruth Brocklehurst, Jane Chisholm & Abigail Wheatley

The publishers are grateful to the following for permission to reproduce material:
Page 44: © Stockbyte/Getty Images (the Moon); Page 60: © SOHO/ESA/NASA/Science Photo Library (the Sun); Page 62: © NASA, ESA, and the Hubble Heritage Team (STScI/AURA) (the Tarantula Nebula); Page 67: © NASA, ESA, G. Illingworth, D. Magee, and P. Oesch (University of California, Santa Cruz), R. Bouwens (Leiden University), and the HUDF09 Team (Hubble 'deep field' group of galaxies).
Every effort has been made to trace and acknowledge ownership of copyright. If any rights have been omitted, the publishers offer to rectify this in any subsequent editions following notification.

This edition first published in 2020 by Usborne Publishing Limited, 83-85 Saffron Hill, London EC1N 8RT, United Kingdom. usborne.com Copyright © 2015, 2016, 2017, 2018, 2019, 2020 Usborne Publishing Limited. The name Usborne and the Balloon logo are registered Trade Marks of Usborne Publishing Limited. All rights reserved. No part of this publication may be reproduced, stored in a retrieval system, or transmitted in any form or by any means without the prior permission of the publisher. First published in America in 2020. This edition published in 2025. UE.